A FEW GOOD THOUGHTS

An Essential Manual for everyday living

By
AYODELE OLUSANYA

authorHOUSE®

AuthorHouse™ UK Ltd.
500 Avebury Boulevard
Central Milton Keynes, MK9 2BE
www.authorhouse.co.uk
Phone: 08001974150

First published by AuthorHouse 11/5/2007

ISBN: 978-1-4343-2904-2 (sc)

Printed in the United States of America
Bloomington, Indiana

This book is printed on acid-free paper.

CONTENTS

INTRODUCTION	I
ACKNOWLEDGEMENTS	III
THOUGHTS – TOPICALLY ARRANGED	1
Action	1
Anger	7
Attitude	13
Commitment	27
Consistency	31
Decision	35
Determination	41
Encouragement	47
Fear	55
Focus	61
Forgiveness	73
Gratitude	77
Inadequacies	83
Influence	89
Initiative	95
Joy	99
Leadership	105
Motivation	109
Opportunity	115
Perseverance	121
Persistence	123
Preparation	129

Procrastination 133

Regrets 137

Relationships 143

Reputation 151

Self Development 159

Self Esteem 165

Time 179

Words 187

AND FINALLY **195**

INTRODUCTION

What exactly is this book aimed at achieving? – Its purpose is to encourage and motivate the reader to 'try'.

A very few years ago, I became bit obsessed with making observations of ordinary everyday events and relating whatever catches my attention to everyday living. It might be what someone says in passing to a major news headline or even things that have happened to me in the past. There is always a moral to be picked up from the slightest comment made, to the most epic of movies. Every life experience is a lesson for someone else to learn from.

I picked up a newspaper one day and I read about a book that was to be launched in London. The book was written by a young British man who had been in Africa for a few months. He visited a few countries in the continent and when he got back to England he decided to put his experience in writing. The book is beautifully titled 'Wake up and smell the Fufu' (Fufu being a popular West African dish). What I found fascinating about the book launch was the calibre of people that were to grace the occasion. Important people from all phases of life within London were there, including the mayor of London. One person who was not present was the author himself – he was not there because he was somewhere else. He was one of the victims of the 7/7 bombings in London.

This got me thinking.

The gentleman concerned had a dream; he wanted to put his experience in the continent of Africa in writing for many to read and learn from – especially from the point of view of a non African. He started his ambition and even though he died under terrible circumstances, his work remains forever. So; suppose he had delayed his writing for a bit longer, suppose he had waited another month or year before he put his 'hand to keyboard', suppose he had thought about the cost and hard work involved and decided to leave it for another day – he would have been just another dead man; nothing special. Two years after his death, movers and shakers of society got together to celebrate his work, only because he tried.

I thought to myself, one of the greatest hindrances that prevent us from doing the do-able when we are meant to do them is Procrastination. The man mentioned above is celebrated because he refused to be a victim of procrastination.

This book is all about such 'thoughts' under various titles such as procrastination, focus, commitment, forgiveness, gratitude, opportunity, relationships, influence, self esteem and the list goes on.

There over 100 different 'thoughts' written by the main author and a few contributors who have either willingly or forcefully allowed their articles to form a part of this project. You will pause to meditate, you will laugh, but most of all, the aim of this book is to encourage you to move from 'trying' to 'succeeding' in whatever endeavours you might find yourself involved in.

ACKNOWLEDGEMENTS

I thought it would be a good idea to have other people join me on this project by asking them to contribute their thoughts; so maybe it's a good idea to start off by recognising these wonderfully people individually.

Kolade Ayodele – A friend of about five years, he is especially knowledgeable in God's Word and an eloquent speaker.

Katherine Charles – I once asked her if she regrets working in the same office with me; she gave me a stern look and said 'at least you make me laugh'. She reminds me of one of my strong points; making people laugh.

Ijapari Haman – A beautiful sister with the voice of an angel and the most charming smile imaginable.

Bola Iduoze – I am yet to meet a better encourager of people. A Good Pastor with superb communication skills.

Oluwayomi Ojo – Her comments on my website make me want to go on – I am sure we will meet some day.

Ayoola Olusanya – she knows me more than anyone else does, you'd expect this after being married to me for over ten years.

Olamide Sanni – One of my adopted younger sisters. I got a few lessons on how to write from her.

DJ Sobanjo – Talent flows in his veins – name it and he will get it done.

Folakemi Togunloju - When she told me I was encouraging her, little did she know that I needed to be encouraged; and that is exactly what she was doing at the time.

Ayoola, Anjola and Toni – the peace I have at home has made my life much easier. Having a family like the one I have can only be a good thing.

The members of Gateway Chapel in Kent, UK, are still clapping for me – Thank you.

Katie Bond, Thanks for making me look good.

I thank the Almighty for His Grace.

ONE

ACTION

---

1. In my heart, I am returning their calls

The head and the heart – the things that go on in our heads and hearts are phenomenal.

I strongly believe that if anyone was to put all the wonderful ideas in his head into some form of action, he would be a bit closer to achieving the wonderful purpose for his life. For most of us, it is far more comfortable to think the thinkable, imagine the imaginable, talk the 'talkable', but a bit more difficult to action the actionable.

'Actioning' the 'Actionable'

I called a member of my church a while ago and later on in the week she got round to calling me back. I was surprised she returned my call; she has never returned any of my previous calls. "Sorry" she said. "I always intend to return calls, but I do it in my heart and that is what matters".

That was just a phone call, no damage done – but how many times have we built castles and mansions in our heads and hearts and done nothing physically in relation to our visualisation. In one way or the other we all suffer from the 'I will do it' syndrome. I will start a diet this month; by the end of this month I will start saving money; this year I am going to change my career; by the end of this year I would have learnt a new skill; henceforth I will start being nicer to people; I intend to start praying every morning before I start my daily routines; I have a new business idea that I need to put into reality, and the list goes on…

It really does not matter how magnificent our thoughts are, without any follow up action it is a pure waste of mental energy.

One 'tradition' that I simply cannot put up with is the trend termed 'New Year Resolution'. It is another way of saying 'I will think about doing it towards the end of a period in time, and then I will spend 30 days trying hard to make it happen and then another eleven months planning to start all over again'.

The difference between the dreamer and the achiever is the action taken towards making the dream come true.

It is not always easy to follow up thoughts with action; there may be many factors that will creep in and disrupt the seemingly most perfectly put together plan. Sometimes our environment, those we surround ourselves with and peculiar conditions play a major role in preventing us from putting our thoughts into action. Excuses play a massive part as well. Some will give a good excuse for not filling in an application form for a new job, and where they manage to fill the form in, submitting is another issue altogether.

In order to eradicate the mindset that prevents us from putting action behind our thoughts it is always best to decide to start small. Taking action on the simplest pre-thoughts can go a long way in empowering us to think about bigger things and putting actions behind them. For instance, decide to call at least two people you have not spoken to for a while this week, go out and watch a sports event live rather than on the TV sometime soon, decide to leave home ten minutes earlier than usual at least one day this week, why not wear your wrist watch on your right hand instead of the usual left, or visa versa – trust me no one will arrest you for doing this! Try one of these for a few weeks and encourage yourself to keep the promise you have made to yourself.

By the time you have achieved something that may seem small, but different, you are ready to take a bigger step towards becoming the action man or woman, hence willing to think of setting up a business of some sort and following the plan through, or maybe just returning a phone call!

Remember; to walk on water you need to get out of the boat.

2. Nothing just happens

Putting the right action behind the right thought is precious; even the Bible gives examples of where performing appropriate action is paramount.

According to 2 kings 4: 8-17 NIV in the good book, one day Elisha went to Shunem, and a well-to-do woman was there and she urged him to stay for a meal. So whenever Elisha came by, he stopped at the woman's place to eat.

o   For Elisha to keep coming back to the home of the couple above to eat, the couple must have formed a relationship with him. Remember, it does not matter what you want to achieve in life – you have to achieve it through people. You need to develop good people skills and work on it everyday.

She said to her husband, "I know that this man who often comes our way is a holy man of God.

o   Some people are in our lives for specific assignments, but what a waste of our time and a waste of the time of the person 'sent' it will be if you fail to recognise the function of such people.

"Let's make a small room on the roof and put in it a bed and a table, a chair and a lamp for him. Then he can stay there whenever he comes to us."

o   Once you recognise that someone is in your life to assist you in fulfilling a dream, it will always be a great idea to invest in the life of such people – it helps the process.

One day when Elisha came, he went up to his room and lay down there. He said to his servant Gehazi, "Call the Shunammite." So he called her, and she stood before him. Elisha said to him, "Tell her, 'You have gone to all this trouble for us. Now what can be done for you?

o   Sooner or later your seed will have to work for you. The relationship you have developed and the investment you have put in will ultimately result in speedy support rendered to you when you need it the most.

Can we speak on your behalf to the king or the commander of the army? She replied, "I have a home among my own people." "What can be done for her?" Elisha asked. Gehazi said, "Well, she has no son and her husband is old."

o   Even when you think all hope is lost, when someone is 'sent' specifically to provide the help you need, nothing becomes impossible. It is never too late for that dream to materialise.

Then Elisha said, "Call her." So he called her, and she stood in the doorway. "About this time next year," Elisha said, "you will hold a son in your arms."

"No, my lord," she objected. "Don't mislead your servant, O man of God!"

o   Faith is very much required when it seems that all hope is lost, but the 'God sent' is telling you that everything will be good.

But the woman became pregnant, and the next year about that same time she gave birth to a son, just as Elisha had told her.

o   Guess what, the woman did not become pregnant 'immaculately'. There was some 'action' involved which included the active participation of her husband. It does not really matter what the 'sent' people have contributed – your status will never change until you involve some form of action into the whole process.

There is always a process.

3. Straight from the garden

Trust me! All that emotional and mental torture that you might be currently enduring will someday come to an end. It will not necessarily need prayers or fasting to bring it all to an end. You will one day suddenly wake up from your sleep and your slumber and take the necessary action to end the mistreatment. You might be suffering emotional pain in the hands of your friends, in your marriage, at college, at work, at church or even from your neighbours. It does not matter how much advice or counsel you might have received, the time to say 'enough' will be determined by you and you will determine the time, the place and the how.

A little guy was sitting in a restaurant eating his meal and minding his own business when all of a sudden a great big man came in and -*whack!* – knocked him of his chair and said," That was a karate chop from Korea."

The little guy thought, "*Ouch*! but he got back on his chair and continued eating his meal and minding his business at the same time. Then all of a sudden – *whack!* – the big man knocked him down again and said, "that was a judo chop from Japan".

The little guy had had enough of this, so he left and was gone for about half an hour. When he came back – *whack!* – he knocked the big man down from his chair out and cold! The little man looked at the people around him and said, "when he comes around, tell him that was a crowbar from the garden".

So, who is knocking you down? - or more to the point – when do you say 'enough'.

TWO

ANGER

1. A very annoying noise

There was a fellowship meeting held at our house, and we were to read a scripture from the Good Book; a very familiar scripture from the book of Matthew which ideally should read:

"You have heard that it was said, 'Eye for eye, and tooth for tooth";

However we were reading from a very unique version of bible and the same scripture above was translated as

"You have heard that the Law of Moses says, 'if an eye is injured, injure the eye of the person who did it. If a tooth gets knocked out, knock out the tooth of the person who did it"

Talk about making your point extremely clear!

Sometimes people, things or situations get on your last nerve and all you can think of doing is applying the Law of Moses, as described in the second scripture above. We could pretend for as much as we like to, we could continue to put on an act for as long as the act may last; anger is real and we all get angry from time to time – the way we handle it is what matters. It also doesn't always boil down to injuring the offender's eyes or knocking out their tooth either, because it's not just other human beings that cause you anger – even those things that do not do a lot of talking can get you fuming as well. One of the best ways of dealing with situations that annoy you is to walk away – but if we walk away each time we get angry, we will soon have nothing to walk away from.

An ordinary guy bought his dream executive car, a car he loved so much that it became his little pet and he loved and cared for it with all his heart; I'm sure some of us can identify with this. One day he was driving his lovely car and he could hear a rattling noise coming from somewhere in the interior. Weeks afterwards he could still hear the rather annoying noise despite doing everything possible to locate where it was coming from. One day while driving, the rattling noise started again – and this time he was irritated so much that while driving he started looking into his glove compartment to see if he could find where the noise was coming from. When he looked up he was on the other side of the road with another car coming fast towards him head – on. He had to make a quick swerve to get himself back to the right side of the road – WOAH! That was close; a terrible accident almost happened.

The gentleman had a few options –

1. He could get back on the road and tell himself that the stupid noise was not worth dying for and decide to ignore the noise forever.

2. He had the choice of doing nothing

3. He could decide to get rid of the car and buy another one that will hopefully be 'rattling noise free'.

Loads of choices – but he did something rather selfless and very worthwhile.

He thought to himself; there must be millions of people experiencing similar annoying noises in their cars and they must get very frustrated driving around listening to the mysterious sound. Then he had another brain wave – what if there was a way of detecting where the rattling was coming from while cars are stationary. A lot of lives might just be saved.

Bingo! A new product called 'Rattle Buster' was born - a product that made the man in question richer than he had ever expected to be.

Using your anger to your advantage!

o   You should not always tolerate what makes you angry – because what you tolerate will never change which means that you might continue to be angry for as long as you live.
o   You cannot afford to do nothing about what upsets you – things will only get worse
o   You cannot afford to discard everyone or everything that upsets you – otherwise you will soon be left with no one and nothing to get rid of.

The best way of dealing with whatever annoys you is using the situation to your advantage; turn your anger into your drive – you will come out at the other end a better person and maybe richer as well!

2.   Get off my stage

There are certain attributes that usually come across as negative when mentioned; one of them being Anger. As controversial as it may sound, anger is not the most atrocious trait to possess; actually I sometimes wish I could get a bit angrier and go the extra mile by showing that I am actually angry. It's not a bad way to be – trust me! If you do not display your displeasure when you need to, people will take you for granted because that is what people do.

However; walking around with a face that makes you look like you've just sucked on some bitter lemon will make people want to run away from you; having the look of Sylvester Stallone in Rambo II most of the time will not win you many friends.

Striking the balance – this is where the need to be friendly but also having a "do not mess with me" demeanour comes in.

Remember the saying – nice guys come last; actually they do. The logic is simple really. "Don't worry about him; he will not mind if we overlook him; he is such a nice guy". And Mr Nice guy gets passed over again and again until there is nothing left to pass by him by.

One of the first things I did when I started at the Polytechnic so many years ago was join the Reggae club. By the time I was in my final year I became the president of the club. Now, if you know me, you might be wondering how a man with my type of manner could lead a bunch of reggae loving brothers and sisters; I used to wonder how I got there myself. One of the main activities we had in the club were open air shows. We would have huge speakers in an open area blasting out reggae tunes and the highlights of such events would be when the 'bubblers' get on stage to dish out some entertaining lyrics – gone are the days! Anyway, there were a few very talented guys who were natural crowd pleasers, they would climb the stage and immediately get the crowd going. These guys for some reason, maybe arrogance, would not join the club but they turned up at our events and they always took centre stage.

We were having one such event and we pulled a massive crowd, I mean hundreds of people came to see us do our thing. I was a bit thirsty from running around trying to ensure that the day went well and I went to the closest bar to get myself big glass of coke. I met one of the extremely talented 'bubblers' who refused to join the club in the bar. He was blabbing his mouth off telling whoever could listen how futile the Reggae club was. He went ahead to say that if it was not for guys like him no one would want to watch the shows we put together. Even when he saw me, the 'top man' standing right in front of him, he would not stop boasting. I walked out of the bar to join my team and about an hour later something rather interesting happened. I saw the guy, yes the same guy come over to the DJ to request a microphone; he was going to mount the stage. I pretended not to notice him; once he got on stage, I ordered the DJ to turn the music off, I climbed the stage and in front of the massive crowd, I ordered him to get off my stage.

Everyone was stunned; my members could not believe what was happening. The guy was truly shocked but I could not be stirred; he was not going to promote his talent via a club he slated just a few minutes ago. He went away with his fellow 'superstars' and the show continued and it went down very well without them – but the episode did not end there.

The next day while on my way for lectures, the same guy I kicked off the stage saw me from afar; he ran towards me and told me that he was sorry for disrespecting the club. To cut the long story short, for the first time of knowing each other for years, we actually became 'friends' and mutual respect reigned.

It's not about the friendship, it's more about the respect that he showed me afterwards; the respect that was non-existent before he made me angry.

Anger when used appropriately would let everyone concerned know what you will tolerate and what you won't; the appropriate use of anger will draw respect your way. People who respond to stressful situations with short-term anger or indignation have a sense of control and optimism that is lacking in those who respond with fear. On the very other hand, anger is damaging when it disrupts our thinking, when we use it to always defend ourselves, harm others and develop an identity as an angry person.

So go on; display your anger when the need be – but use your anger wisely because a fool gives full vent to his anger, but a wise man keeps himself under control (Proverbs 29:11).

THREE

ATTITUDE

---

1. Do you need a tissue?

I usually drive to work, but on this particular Friday I had to get the train because I was going to see a special event after work and I didn't really fancy driving all the way to the venue. Apart from that, I always jump at the opportunity to take public transport – it always means that I leave the driving to someone else while I make time to read or maybe doze off.

Fortunately for me, my station is the starting point of the train for the 50 minutes ride into London. This meant that I was able to pick and choose my seat and I picked a really nice spot hoping for a peaceful ride. The three seats next to me where soon to be filled up; three ladies sat around me and one who must be in her early twenties was chatting on her phone even before she took her seat. O my God! I thought. It's going to be one of those days, here I was trying to read and opposite me was Miss Chatterbox. And true to my judgement, she chatted for almost ever. She would tell whoever she was talking to that she had to switch over to another caller on her phone; as one call ended, she made another one. I did not aim to notice all this, but you would have to be blind or deaf, or maybe both not to take notice of the young lady with the phone.

I was determined to finish the chapter I was reading and this meant that I had to try hard not to get distracted by the rather popular lady. But being human, once in a while I would look up at the lady and I would think of her as a rather selfish person who could not bother to respect other people's will to have peace. I thought of her as a needy person who had to talk to the whole world in order to create the illusion that she is important. It did not end there; while she continued to distract me I would look up once in a while and wonder what poor man would put up with this blabbermouth.

After a little thought, I would go back to my reading but her ranting would again make me look up. I just did not like her.

My opinion about the young lady was about to change.

I looked up again and I noticed the lady had tears running down her cheeks. I could see that she was trying hard to disguise the tears but her eyes were ever so red. She was obviously distressed over something. Everyone noticed she was crying but no one said anything to her. I had a packet of tissues in my pocket and I handed one to her; not because she necessarily needed it, but because she could do with some sympathy.

Hold on a minute – how did my emotion change from 'what a nuisance' to 'poor girl' in a matter of seconds. Where did the switch in attitude come from?

I judged her – I had already concluded within myself the type of person I thought she was, and it was not a very good picture.

Before you judge me, I need to tell you in no uncertain terms that we are all guilty of this rather unfortunate trait. We all judge other people either consciously or otherwise. We judge others by the way they dress, talk, their class and position in life, the job they do, who they marry, how they look, where they live and the list goes on. If you are still in denial, the next time you meet someone for the first time, listen to yourself think. The first few thoughts in your head are the 'judgement thoughts', we all have these thoughts – however the difference is in the delay factor.

Delay your judgement of other people. The whole world is always in a hurry to get somewhere and everyone is trying to outrun the other in the rat race of life. The impact of this is manifested in our thinking and judgement of others which is too fast most of the time. You cannot like everyone, let's not get hypocritical about things, just like everybody cannot like you, but you can at least take your time in making your mind up about others. It would be took a minute to judge slowly and to give others a chance before we start using our head to put them into labelled boxes.

If I could rewind – once the Chatterbox lady (she was chatting; this fact cannot be denied) came to sit next to me, I would first think to myself "why here? Does she like me or something?" Then I would say to myself, "she must have something urgent to say for her to be calling the whole world this early". This will reduce the potential of wrong judgement; then when the crying started – I would have thought to myself "I was right", and then offer her the tissue.

2. From us to you

The next day was going to be a very significant day in my life; it was going to be forty years since I came into this beautiful world. So there I was in the office, my eyes glued to the monitor while my hands were typing away and my mind was fixed on the letter I was desperately trying to complete before it was home time. Out of the blue, bang! There was an envelop on my desk – followed by a beautiful voice belonging to a colleague, "this is a present from everyone in the office to you on the occasion of your birthday".

I smiled and then continued with my work, even though by this time I was wondering why; why oh why!

Just a few days before all this someone else in the office was about to turn forty, I organised a very elaborate presentation which involved everyone in the office gathering around and the Regional Director presenting the gift we got for the celebrant. A few weeks earlier a much younger lady was also celebrating her birthday and I arranged a 'proper' presentation for her, so there I was continuing to wonder why my present was dumped on my desk as if I was some irrelevant about to be forty years young man!

I eventually got out of my seat, walked to my managers' office and asked her to come to the general office and present my gift to me 'properly' – and she did.

I know exactly what you are thinking!

'What an arrogant so and so, does it matter how you get the gift, at least they contributed money and bought you something and you should be grateful'. You know what, I am grateful and I love my colleagues so much for the very expensive gift they got me. Actually I am flattered because I don't think anyone else has been so magnificently honoured in terms the money the office must have put together. And do you know what; I got presents from my current and former colleagues as well, so I have reasons to be thankful. However, it is not about the gift.

I know that the world never gives you what you deserve; you only get what you 'demand', in the same vain you will only be treated the way you ask to be treated. The intriguing thing about demanding to be treated in particular ways is that your demand does not always have to be vocal. I have never met anyone with a sign post on the forehead saying 'treat me with respect', however; there are people who walk around with an invisible tag that says 'don't mess with me' expressed by their body language. Whichever style suits you, you have to let people know what you will tolerate and express this adequately and quickly.

Winning the popularity contest – the main reason why some of us would rather smile while we are being addressed or treated inappropriately rather than voice our true feelings. We accommodate the hurt and go home to cry to mama. Too many of us would rather play happy go merry so that hopefully we will be looked at as being nice natured. Unfortunately, it never works. By enduring anything that is thrown our way we end up losing any form of respect and then become another 'nice guy', you know the type, they always come last. People would rather know exactly where you stand, what you will accept and actions you see as unacceptable. You don't have to shout 'respect me' wherever you go, but you need to allow your quiet voice of discontent or approval to heard quickly by all concerned – you will be treated well for it.

That explains why I wanted my colleagues to know how I wanted to receive the gift, I demanded to be treated with some decorum, because I am worth it – I am sure you are worth it as well.

You cannot afford to go through life accepting everything and anything that is thrown your way. You have been carefully put together by the creator; you need to remember on a daily basis that you are fearfully and wonderfully made, and you need to know this fully well (Psalm 139:14)

3. I decided differently – Contributed by Folakemi Togunloju

As I have gotten older, I now understand the saying; "older and wiser" better. It is not necessarily true that one is wise just because they are older.

The saying comes from the fact that as one gets older, chances are that they might have made a few mistakes and learnt from them; hence getting wiser. We have to make the decision to learn from past mistakes else the opportunity to learn is wasted. Most times it is easy to sit and cry and lament on our mistakes but the most stress free option is to learn from it and put it behind us.

It is easier said than done, but when we make the decision to be positive each day regardless of what happens it is amazing the amount of positive things that start to happen. One day I woke up after getting tired of lamenting and thinking of all the mistakes I had made. I decided to start my day with a simple prayer. The prayer went; "God I thank you for giving me the privilege to wake up on this beautiful day and as I step out of my house I pray that regardless of what happens I'll choose to see the positive side of things. I choose not to get angry or upset. I choose to smile even when things get me down. I choose to use positive words and better still I pray I put a smile on someone's face. I can say that on that particular day towards the end of work, my colleagues were quite convinced I had won the lottery or something. I thought, is it that easy to have a positive day because I chose to? The answer is yes, but obviously the bigger the challenge we face, the harder that choice becomes, but we have to persist.

Living a positive and fulfilled life is about praying to God to give us the wisdom to make the right choices.

4. keeping your mind busy

I usually leave work at a bit after 5pm every weekday. I cannot afford the luxury of staying too late because I have to pick up my girls from their after school club and nursery which are about 10 minutes from each other; however the drive from work to my first port of call, the after school club is very unpredictable. The journey could last from between one hour, to 90 minutes depending on the weight of traffic. My wife works further away from home and she is never back in good enough time to pick the girls up, hence the responsibility always lies on me.

On a particular Wednesday the traffic was a bit horrendous to put it mildly. I was stuck in traffic for what seemed to be eternity. To make matters worse, my personal mobile phone was very low on battery power and I knew it was only a matter of time before it went dead. And as if that was not bad enough, my work mobile phone refused to work. My wife called me and I explained my predicament, I managed to tell her that I was about 12 miles away from the after school club, I told her my phone will go off any minute, and I also said that at the current tempo of traffic movement, the chances of me getting to the after school club and nursery before they close was tending towards zero. Then the phone went dead!

So there I was, stuck in traffic, with no means of communication and with no possibility of getting to pick the girls up on time – what a dilemma. I was fuming, my blood pressure went up drastically and I began to get agitated. Then I decided to talk to myself, saying calm down; relax my friend; your hyperventilation will not make any difference to the traffic nor the dead phones. And for once I listened to myself – I decided not to get myself worked up and instead I started to think about how I was going to be spending Christmas. It was not very easy to divert my thinking but I did it.

There are some circumstances that we find ourselves in and there is nothing we can do to influence the situation. We then spend time and effort worrying and getting ourselves worked up and stressed out. At a point in life we are all faced with situations that we might not necessarily like, however we will have to accept them. If there is the slightest chance that we could change the situation, then each individual owes himself the duty of vigorously pursuing the needed change of circumstances. There is no point in grumbling about your boss at work when you have two clear options to choose from. You could either get the boss executed, or look for another job (I recommend the latter). Sometimes the circumstances might be very drastic and not very pleasant; but seriously, would you rather let the particular situation put a stop to the rest of your life or would you rather dust yourself up and get busy thinking of how to manage the rest of your life. I read somewhere that many of the successful people have had to overcome some very difficult times and situations. As a matter of fact, what had made them successful was their ability to overcome unpleasant situations.

Imagine; if Mr Lincoln had given up his dream when he lost the senate seat, the United States would have been denied one of the finest Presidents. I wonder what would have happened if he had spent his energy lamenting over his failing, rather than on ways of rectifying the situation.

Oh yeah! Back to my situation in that awful traffic, I eventually got to the after school club at 6.50pm, and guess what – strangely, my wife got to the girls before their schools closed. I wonder what would have happened if I had been so stressed out while in the traffic that I was involved in an accident out of frustration; only to get home to find out that everything was ok.

Rather than getting stressed; get thinking!

5. Like that wasn't enough

Things that life throws at us!

Earlier on in the year, our dear Minister of Finance in the UK, otherwise called the Chancellor of the Exchequer gave his annual budget for the coming financial year. By the time he was done I broke into a very cold sweat. The Chancellor wants me to pay twice what I pay now on my car tax, how on earth does he expect me to balance my already unbalanced books? I mean, things are so tight that I haven't been able to afford the new Playstation 3 console and when I asked the 'wifey' to chip in to help raise funds to buy the console she threatened to throw a punch.

Like that wasn't enough, I was trying to get fit earlier in the week and during the vigorous exercise I fell awkwardly and broke my left wrist leaving me in pure pain all week long. Again as if that was not enough, driving to work everyday in the last week could best be described as a nightmare. Each day I got to work or home I had to check the car round just to make sure the words 'stupid driver' were not inscribed anywhere on the body of the car. Other drivers just took pleasure in cutting in front of me without showing any form of acknowledgement and each time this happened I felt blood rushing to my head in full speed. Like that was not enough, I expended too much energy this week sorting out relational problems between a Team Leader and a member of her team; again draining the little will power I had left out of me. Then Friday came, and I thought, thank God the week is finally ending, only to get home from work to see my baby girl covered in itchy spots and she had a very high temperature for company; apparently some chicken gave her the spots – all in one week but despite my rather very awkward week, one thing I know for sure is that 'Life is good'!

I know loads of other people would have had even worse weeks, maybe months or maybe years far worse than the week that I am whinging about.

Life sometimes seems to just love throwing issues at us whenever it feels like it. Things could be going ok-ish when suddenly 'Bang!' a nasty blow appears from nowhere. The blow could come from people, situations, or circumstances and sometimes they come from all of the above. The most intriguing thing about the 'blow' we sometimes encounter is that we have no control whatsoever over them. I mean, it is entirely up to the Chancellor how much he wants me to pay for my car tax; I cannot influence how other drivers decide to drive their cars; the wrist is already bust, I wish I could put the thing back in place but it requires a bit more than a quick fix; I wish I could have asked the 'chicken' to stand clear of my daughter, but the thing just wouldn't have listened anyway.

I have little or no influence over some of the things that I experienced in the past week; however I have full control over how I choose to respond to each situation. That is the difference in the results we get in life; our response in dealing with what life throws at us.

Imagine that I challenged one of the drivers who decided to cut in front of me, imagine that I got out my car, imagine that he got out of his, imagine that he turned out to be a massive muscular guy with a baseball bat in his hand and smoke coming out of his ear holes and nostrils, imagine that he beat the living daylight out of my rather skinny self, imagine that I had to be lifted home in an helicopter because no hospital is equipped enough to mend me – so what exactly would I do to stop my wife from looking at me thinking she married a wimp?

Come to think off, I think I did the right thing by giving the bad drivers a good telling off in my 'head', and going back home with my body intact – innit?

Remember, it is not so much about what life throws at you, but how well, or otherwise you handle the situation.

6. Only new in the business

It can be quite daunting, actually I think it is sometimes discouraging when you compare yourself with other people who have been in your particular profession or career for much longer that you have. You sometimes compare yourself to someone and wish you had started in that particular field much earlier. Have you ever almost regretted studying a particular course in college because you have now looked back and wished that you had studied something else? Maybe you studied Mathematics & Statistics and later found yourself in the field of project management – you would have started in your new line of work much earlier, acquired a lot more experience and maybe moved much higher up on the ladder if you had studied something else you might wonder. Where you had spent 5 years adding figures, you could have had a further 5 years experience in your new career. However; I know for sure that the race is not to the swift or the battle to the strong, nor does food come to the wise or wealth to the brilliant or favour to the learned; but time and chance happen to them all (Ecclesiastes 9:11).

How do I know this you may ask? We had a guest around the other week and I was engaging him in a conversation when suddenly there was a clip from an interview involving the special one on TV. Our guest said something rather interesting – he said "do you know Jose Mourinho (the special one) has never played professional football before". Really I shouted. You could be astonished by my ignorance but the thought that the 'special one' had never ever played professional football surprised me – why?

In the UK especially, and across the rest of the world, every top football manager was once a professional footballer. Actually; it is considered a top criterion for every manager to have at one time or the other in their lives played the beautiful game.

The first thing that I did after I heard the bombshell was to 'Google' Mr Mourinho and below was what I found on the website '4thegame.com', about the special one.

"The son of famous Portugal goalkeeper Felix Mourinho, Jose never played professionally. He first came into the spotlight as Bobby Robson's translator at Sporting Lisbon in the early 1990s, having held low-profile positions at Portuguese clubs Estrela Amadora and Vitoria Setubal prior to that".

Eh! I thought – just a translator only over the last decade; now leading one of the top clubs in Europe (or maybe in the world). He is now considered to be a much better manager compared to those 'well experienced' bosses who had formally played international football and won loads of titles during their time. The managers who had been in the 'business' for much longer and acquired much more experience, in present day football take the second place to the special one despite all their knowledge.

This has really encouraged me. I used to see those who have been writing for longer than myself as idols and I always believed that I would never reach their standard, at least not until I am old and grey and maybe with a walking stick. I would read some articles and wonder 'My God! Will I ever be this good? But not anymore; now I know that all that is required is the right attitude and the grace of the Almighty and I would reach the greatest height of my chosen endeavour in no time. I still see other writers as people I could learn from, but in the same light I know I could reach their height in a very very short time.

So can you. Even if you had only just decided to pick up a new career at a later stage of your life; even if you had only just started to learn sometime new; even if you have feel intimidated by the experienced ones – all you need to do is remember that race is not to the swift; remember to develop the right attitude and put your trust and believe in the God you serve – then just relax because you are going in the right direction to becoming the special one in your chosen field.

7. The illegal immigrant

A man arrived in America many years ago. He was originally from the Netherlands and he out stayed his welcome in the US. Officially he was an illegal immigrant, subject to various immigration controls which meant that there was only so much he could get up to while he remained in the country. His immigration status would prevent him from getting a decent job, prevent him from starting a business, and buying a house would be an uphill task.

The man, who many people called Colonel, had some form of restriction that would have prevented him from doing anything meaningful with his life while he was in America. His constraint was his legal status in the country – yours and mine could be something else. True greatness is achieved when you can overcome whatever hindrances threaten to hold you down, be it physical, mental, situational, relational, financial, or positional. It is very convenient to drum up excuses; we can give all the excuses under the sun for why we cannot perform particular tasks – tasks and actions that could make us stand out and achieve greatness; the greatness that will fail to manifest until we decide to look beyond whatever our constraints or restrictions might be, and endeavour to break through regardless.

All we need to do is look around, look closely enough and there will always be someone who we can point to; someone who has disregarded the limiting factor in his or her life and forged ahead and got 'the job done'. The difference between those who get up and go despite what their circumstances might be, and those who don't is the power of a Positive Mental Attitude.

There are some people who allow their conditions and circumstances determine how much they get out of life, and there are others who determine what they will get out of life despite their conditions and circumstances. The latter are more energetic, positive and they always live life to the fullest.

Many of us spend too much time, way too much time wallowing on our wish list. I wish I had more money; if only I was better looking; if only I could change my accent; I wish I was not born with this medical condition; I wish I had a better handwriting; if only I had a better singing voice; if only I had the right papers to work in this country – and that brings me back nicely to the illegal immigrant.

Recently the world celebrated thirty years since the passing away of one of the greatest musical legends that lived. Just over thirty years ago the world lost the King of Rock 'n' Roll, Elvis Presley. Elvis was, and still is a household name all over the world. Despite Elvis's success, he never performed outside the United States. Do you know why? - for every successful entertainer, there must be a good manager, a manager who will bring out the best in the performer while ensuring that maximum financial returns are in the bank. Obviously, Elvis had a top manager, a guy referred to as Colonel – but the Colonel was an illegal immigrant in America; and if Elvis was to perform outside America, the Colonel would not be allowed back into the country.

I am sure that the Colonel was not the only illegal immigrant during his time, but while some of this fellow foreigners where spending time worrying about their status and feeling disadvantaged while doing whatever jobs they could lay their hands on – the Colonel spent his time doing what he knew how to do best – managing. I am sure that the thought of his status in the country would have popped up in his head from time to time, but his attitude would have been "I cannot influence my legal status, but at least I can manage, and managing I will do well" – and he did, despite his funny spoken English.

The time has come, the time for us to get our abilities and our talents into full use and pay less attention to the disadvantages that we have. Life is about choices – we have the choice to concentrate on what we are good at; the choice to pay attention to what our strengths are - and pay less attention to what we can do very little about. Everyone owes it to themselves to choose wisely.

8. The real difference maker – Story provided by Lyn Craddock

What makes a man (or woman) stand out?

We all happen to be human beings, but as it happens some stand out more than others and this has nothing to do with how rich or poor you are, it is non-dependant on your social standing or how educated you are. What truly marks out very few out from the many rest is the positive impact these very few have had in the life of those they come intact with.

There are some people who have chosen (yes it's a choice) to have an impact on others and these people stand out because they are usually happy, content, influential and others want to be around them. These few are the difference makers.

A typical example of this is Mr Bertie Charles Joseph Craddock.

Mr Craddock was married for just four months when he had to leave the arms of his newly wed wife and travel to a far land as an army officer. Unfortunately for Mr Craddock, Singapore, where he was serving, fell to the Japanese and he, along with many other British solders became a prisoner of war for over 3 years. During this rather horrid time of his life he was made to work hard to help build the Burma railway; he fed on three small bowls of 'maggot infested' rice a day; suffered tropical diseases such as malaria, beriberi and dysentery. He had to exchange his wedding ring for food just to stay alive. He was beaten regularly and he only just avoided getting electrocuted.

He was not alone in this predicament; there were others going through the same dilemma and many died from various diseases, starvation, loneliness and torments. Sometimes, Mr Craddock would wake up and find out that his pal lying beside him was dead. He would have to take body after body and dump them on a fire – to save them from the indignity of decaying under the soaring heat. But, while others were going through the rather difficult times feeling dejected and crumbling under the strain – Mr Craddock decided to stand out; he was a difference maker at the Singapore 'hell'.

So what exactly did he do?

He kept a small picture of his wife pinned to his bed space, he would regularly look at the picture and then look at the moon and say to himself that his wife was looking at the same moon. He would constantly sing happy songs and tell funny stories, in the process dragging many others to his bed space giving them a moment of happiness despite the suffering. He managed to keep a happy face and this brightened the heart of all those who he came in contact with despite the hard times. While many grumbled, he made a decision to stay positive and be an encourager of other soldiers, constantly reminding them that there is a better future just around the corner even though the so called better times seemed oblique at the period.

He made a difference in the life of other prisoners of war and in the process he stayed alive to be reunited with his wife and to live the rest of his life in true happiness.

We all find ourselves in very uncomfortable situations from time to time. It might be at work, in family circumstances, or in our social surroundings. How we react to situations has a positive or negative impact on those who come our way. If you decide to go about your business with a positive attitude and a good heart, others will be blessed by your magnificence and people will want to be around you. Your attitude is a matter of choice that only you can make – a decision to make the best of your current situation, learn from it, carry others along and get blessed; or a decision to wallow in self pity and walk around feeling dejected and being a negative impact on all concerned.

The decision is yours, but I want to challenge you to be the difference maker; just for a while at least!

FOUR

COMMITMENT

1. I am being invaded

In my head, it was never going to happen – but the day came and there was a knock on the door. They came with tools and materials and what I have dreaded for months was just about to happen.

It was a few months ago that my wife, Ayoola told me that she was going to redecorate the house, the whole of it. For what exactly, I asked; as far as I could see the house is in a good condition, the decoration is fine and the everybody seems to be happy with the way things are – so why the bother? More so, the cost! I did everything I could think of to persuade her to please reconsider. I even threatened to move out of the house during the time of the works if it was to go ahead. She looked at me straight in the eyes when I told her this and she said in a very calm tune "brilliant idea, but you might have to stay wherever you go forever". With that remark she made her point very clear; but I didn't stop there. I even told her that we would be disrupting the lives of the kids if the works were to go ahead but I was still ignored.

You see, everything I told my wife were mere excuses; deep down I had other reasons why I really did not want the works to go ahead. It was not the cost (she hadn't asked me for money YET!). It was not any of the reasons above – it was simply because I could not bear the inconvenience I would have to endure during the works. I mean I would not be able to play on the Playstation for weeks; I would not be able to watch my favourite TV programmes in the convenience of my living room. The conservatory turned 'study' would be a no go area – how on earth would I do my reading and writing? The internet connection will be disrupted; I will not be able to listen to music while I work, my bedroom will be so turned over that

I will struggle to find what to wear for weeks, the kitchen will become a no go area which will mean that there will be no home cooking for weeks – HELP!

Sounds familiar?

Not the redecoration of the house; I mean the inconvenience that you might have to face if you really want to make a difference to your own dear life.

Imagine wanting to take a big step in your life.

Maybe it's time to change your career; maybe it's a business idea that keeps popping up in your head; maybe you desire to change some horrible habits you have; maybe it's time to relocate; maybe it's time to learn something new; or maybe, just maybe it's time to put some action behind that vision that has remained a vision for as long as you can remember. You know the step needs to be taken, but you are comfortable with the way things are now and there is no immediate reason for you to rock the boat which means that the need to change anything can wait another day, wait another week, it could wait another month, it could wait another few years, it might as well wait until it is too late – what is the hurry, at least you are comfortable with the way things are currently.

One of the main enemies of commitment is convenience; they never see eye to eye, and they are not meant to.

If you cannot let go of your present convenience, even temporarily, then you will always have a problem when it comes to committing to achieving a real life changing goal. Any real achievement will come with a degree of inconvenience; and if you commit yourself to making a difference, a degree of inconvenience will have to be endured.

A friend of mine had to leave his family behind for weeks while he travelled to South Africa to get some training – commitment to improve his skills vs. convenience of staying with the family; Bear Grylls had to feed on raw meat from dead animals for weeks in his quest to become the youngest British climber ever to reach the summit of Mount Everest and return alive – commitment to make history vs. convenience of eating burger at McDonalds. Chris Gardner had to suffer the inconvenience of sleeping in a public toilet with his young son on his way to becoming a self-made millionaire, entrepreneur, motivational speaker and philanthropist – commitment to becoming so great that that a movie was made about his life vs. the convenience of a good nights sleep.

Endure the inconveniences; actually embrace them and remember – the harder the battle, the sweeter the victory.

2. That nail belongs to me

About 500 years ago, Spanish explorer Hernando Cortez sailed into the harbour of Vera Cruz, Mexico with just 600 men and yet over the next two years his vastly outnumbered forces were able to defeat Montezuma and all the warriors of the Aztec empire, making Cortez the conqueror of all Mexico.

This was a great feat especially when two prior expeditions involving thousands of men each time had failed to establish a colony on Mexican soil. Mr. Cortez knew that he and his men had an almost impossible task in front of them, but he was not going to be crushed. He knew that the road before them would be dangerous and difficult, and he knew that his men would be tempted to ditch their quest and 'do a runner' back Spain. And so, as soon as Cortez and his men had come ashore and unloaded their provisions, he ordered their entire fleet of eleven ships to be destroyed. His men stood on the shore and watched as their only possibility of retreat burned and sank. And from that point on, they knew beyond any doubt there was no return, no turning back. Nothing lay behind them but an empty ocean, which meant that their only 'choice' was to go forward, to conquer or die – a phenomenon otherwise called 'commitment'.

Conversely, many years ago in the good land of Haiti, a certain man was desperate to sell his house for two thousand dollars and another man was desperate to purchase the house. After a great deal of negotiating the owner of the house agreed to sell his house for half of the original amount, not because the buyer could not afford the asking price, but he wanted to take advantage of the sellers desperation and make some saving. However one condition had to be met. The original owner would still own one nail that hung over the home's front door. The agreement was made and the sale of the house was completed.

After a few years the original owner of the house wanted to buy the house back but the new owner refused to sell. So the first owner went out and found the carcass of a dead dog and hung it on the nail that he still owned in the house. Before long the house became unliveable due to the stench from the unhealthy guest hanging on the front door, so much so that the family was forced to sell the house to the owner of the nail.

While Mr Cortez was committed to his mission and achieved with a few men what thousands could not accomplish, the new buyer of the house above could not commit his full finances to what was supposedly his dream home, thus eventually ending up losing the house.

Your success or otherwise in any endeavour is directly proportional to you level of commitment to such venture. There will always be times when you want to give up the fight and go back home, you are not alone when it comes to being discouraged sometimes and even getting frustrated by the seemingly delay in getting your desired results despite the incredible efforts you have put in. I happen to hold the equivalent to a masters degree when it comes to wanting to sometimes jump from my bedroom window in frustration – I guess this explains why the missus put up some fanciful blinds on the bedroom window, giving strict instructions that I ensure the blinds are not damaged in my attempt to jump!

Commitment – it keeps you from looking back; being committed to a task gives you the drive to keep moving forward despite what life may throw at you, when you are committed you reduce the number of choices you have and put your full resources and focus into making sure that your dreams comes true. When the 'wise men' come with the aim of telling you that you are getting a bit too ambitious for your own good, your commitment to the course gives you the will to carry on without looking back.

Your commitment to succeed at any task that you have decided to embark on should never wear; you owe yourself the duty of putting the right infrastructures in place in your life to ensure that the resolve to thrive never dwindles, otherwise the man who owns the nail may want to hang a dead dog over your dream house.

FIVE

CONSISTENCY

---

1. A very clean car

I was driving in the slow lane on one of the busiest motorways with my music pumping really loud and my mind wondering all over the place with various thoughts. The weather was not particularly great, it was cloudy and the road was wet. I looked into my side mirror and there was a car about to go past me, it kind of stood out. It wasn't particularly extraordinary, but while most cars were looking rather dirty, due to the weather, this car was extremely clean (I have a thing for clean cars). Once it went past me I realised why it looked so immaculate. It had the brand new registration number on it which reminded me that the date was the 1st March, the day when a set of brand new cars with the newest registration numbers are released in the UK.

"How great!" I thought. Since 1st September, 2001, the UK has implemented a system whereby every 1st day of March and 1st day of September new cars with corresponding registration numbers are released into the market without fail – how consistent!

For the next hour of driving I got thinking about the importance of consistency in my life and I guess it's rather crucial in your life as well. I mean what exactly do you stand for, and how often do we allow various factors stir us away from what we truly believe in?

The fortitude of inconsistency blinds us from reaching the destiny that we sometimes set for ourselves because the slightest form of distraction makes us deviate in a hurry into doing things that we should have no business with in the first place. Even the good book refers to such people as 'unstable in all they do' (James 1:8). The symptoms of inconsistency include giving up rather too easily, negative experiences becoming a good reason to rethink the whole process, getting carried away by temporary excitements hence taking our eyes off the long term bigger picture, being vulnerable to other people's opinion. Inconsistency makes us come across as unreliable and this could lead us to being termed as untrustworthy.

I need to stress that I am very much in favour of change, but change that is necessary to enhance progress and not change for the sake of changing.

We all need to pride ourselves in whatever we stand for; this will draw respect from all and sundry. If you manage to kick my head while I am deep in sleep and ask me what my dreams and aspirations are, apart from me beating the living day light out of you for waking me up in such manner, I will not have to think twice before I start blabbing about the same things I have been blabbing about for the past 5 years, at least. If circumstances force me to change direction so be it, but in the meantime I will consistently continue to pursue my dream relentlessly.

You will notice that people who decide to pursue certain courses and stick to them despite any odds, usually come out on top. They make their mark not just because they eventually achieve their heart desires but more so because they die fighting for what they believe in, leaving behind a legacy. The most famous man living today is Nelson Mandela. He knew what he wanted, went all the way trying to get it and even 27 years of imprisonment could not dampen his spirit. If that isn't consistency – then what is?

So how can we promote consistency in our lives?

Do you truly believe in it, do you visualise yourself getting it, will it truly make you happy and fulfilled, will it be beneficial to others than yourself and your immediate family? – Yes?

Then get consistent!

2. Then David killed Goliath

What styles are you really comfortable with when it comes to getting things that matter to you done?

Have you ever consciously recognised who you are, accepted who you are and have you consistently continued to be you, or do you consistently do what the world expects you to do, the way the world expects you to do things?

There is so much pressure on us to do things the way that we might not necessarily be comfortable with, and those who stick to doing things in a manner that they feel comfortable with are accused of not being flexible enough to change. Change – what change? While change might be a good thing when applied appropriately, there are times when I just want to do things in a particular way because that is the way I like to do such things and the rest of the world should leave me alone and let me get on with myself.

Except while on vacation or when I have committed myself to some activity, I spend my Sunday afternoons in bed sleeping and I love that. You might think that I am lazy and rather than sleeping I should be spending my time doing something constructive like spending time with the family or washing the car – but I am not interested in such things on Sunday afternoons, all I want to do is sleep for hours. I was studying for a diploma and was required to submit my assignments periodically. While some of my fellow students read well ahead of time and submitted their assignments very early, I always left my reading until the last minute and I submitted my assignment on the deadline day. You might think I am not proactive, whereas I think I get a buzz from the last minute rush which I find exciting and it suits me just fine. When I read or write, I have to have music blazing very loud. The bass has to be pumping and at intervals of maybe twenty minutes I have to get up and boogie. This is why I now use earphones; I have to spare the rest of my family my noise. I am sure most people read and write in quiet environments; I can't!

You must have heard the over expressed sentiment "some love it cold, some love it hot" – question; how do you like it?

The speed at which you achieve your desired dream in life is very much dependent on your preferred methods of handling situations. Where you have to adopt other people's methods and techniques, you will end up slowing yourself down. The earlier you recognise your most comfortable method of dealing with people and issues; the earlier you decide to consistently be your own person - then the greater the chances that you will reach the promised land sooner.

Do you know one of the secret weapons used by David in defeating Goliath in the Good Book? He dressed up in his preferred attire and used his preferred weapon! He had consistently dressed up in a particular way and he kept to his comfort zone in defeating the unfriendly giant.

According to 1 Samuel 17: 38 – 39; King Saul gave David his own armour to wear in fighting Goliath. David put it on and took a step or two to see what it was like. After trying them out, David turned to King Saul and said "I can't go in these; I am not used to them". He took the rather uncomfortable armour off and approached Goliath with his preferred Shepherd's bag, equipped with his preferred choice of weapons of five stones, his shepherd's staff and his sling.

I could imagine being in the crowd on the day – I guess I would be shouting "Please David wear the armour, it will protect you". And I can imagine David having the right attitude and shouting back at me "My friend, shut up and mind your mouth otherwise one of these stones will end up knocking out one of your teeth".

Identify your preferred style and consistently develop it to ensure that you use it to get your desired results in life rather quickly.

SIX

DECISION

1. Litmus test - Blended with extracts from a sermon delivered by Bola Iduoze

The decisions we make ultimately determine how we live our lives – the decisions might be considered major i.e. who to marry, how many children to have, what career to pursue, where to live and whom we choose as our friends. Some decisions are minor, decisions as what to wear, whether to go to work today or not, what book to read (or to avoid), what to have for dinner and maybe the decision of who to listen to.

All decisions, either major, minor or somewhere in between will have an impact on our immediate or long-term future. The better the decisions we make, the better the life we live. We make decisions all the time – for instance it is your decision to continue reading this book or to put a stop to it and get something to eat. You will decide later today what time you will be going to bed and what time you will be dragging yourself to the bathroom in the morning.

Some decisions are wrong, some are right – so how do you classify the decision you make even before you commit yourself to it?

Below is the litmus test; a few guiding steps that might just help us decide right.

o   Idea test: What has the Word of God to say about the decision you are about to make? Every major decision you might need to make can be referred back to the Bible, all you need to do is search until you find.

o   Integrity test: As a man of God once said, "If you live in sin, you will enjoy it in darkness". Anything that you do, and you are ashamed for anyone else to know about it, is a bad decision in the making. If you are not comfortable sharing it with anyone, then maybe it's time to put a halt to whatever the thing might be.

o   Improvement test: Will the decision improve you? If it wouldn't, then what exactly is the point? When I decided to go to the gym, it was because I wanted to look and feel better. When I observed that my belly was increasing in size, I decided to stop eating biscuits every night before I went to bed.

o   Independence test: Anything you would get addicted to and find difficult to step away from should be avoided like a plague. Pastor Bola of Gateway Chapel told of how she decided to watch daytime soaps on TV. She would arrange everything that she did (including her prayer time) around the soaps. She had to make an even more difficult but rewarding decision to halt watching the soaps altogether and eventually she got her independence back.

o   Influence test: It's my life – not really. If the decision is going to have a negative impact on those around you, especially those who love you, then maybe you should have a rethink. No one is an island, and everyone has a string of other people that are   associated to them one way or the other. For every selfish decision you make, someone might get badly hurt – the kind of hurt that could be extremely difficult to shake off.

o   Investment test: We have very little control over time. Any decision that will result in a waste of your investment in time should be reconsidered. We have very little of it – we need to use it wisely.

Decisions – where you can, apply the litmus test; it might make a whole heap of 'good' difference.

2. Only because I am not deaf

Have you ever had to repeat yourself over and over again with little or no joy until you have had to do something a bit more drastic to get your point across? This happened to me the other week, except that I was the one on the receiving end. I was the one who had to be taught a bitter lesson, a lesson that I have had to come to terms with, a lesson that I have learnt from, even though it's a bit unfortunate.

Recently, I was blabbing my mouth off on stage during an event and trust me I was already feeling a bit uncomfortable because no one was laughing at my jokes; then suddenly my mobile phone went off. This was a bit strange because nobody would usually call that late in the evening, but what was more worrying was that the phone caused interference with the sound equipment in the hall which was a bit embarrassing. The only good thing was that the phone did not ring out loud because I always have my phone on vibrate mode. The phone was in my pocket and I was holding a microphone – imagine how I would have felt if the phone actually rang out loud. I managed to end the rather embarrassing session and the first thing I wanted to do was find out who on earth was calling me at an awkward time – it was someone I knew and he was actually in the crowd. I asked him why he rang me while I was delivering a speech "I wanted you to finish and leave the stage because you were taking too much time". His point could not have been made any clearer. It was even clearer when I realised that he had told a few people about what he was going to do and no one thought it was out of order.

I want to heed to his suggestion as well; at least give the guy credit – he tried to stop my stage antics, and in all honesty I think I need to improve myself as well so taking a back step would be a good idea. But it still felt a bit saddening.

But come to think of it, why should it be disheartening?

Many times life is about making decisions in rather awkward situations. You will not get encouragement, support or even nice words or deeds from everyone you come across. You cannot afford to let go of whatever you believe in due to a bump in the ride. It is impossible for everyone to treat you the way you would like to be treated and the rest of the world does not have to cheer you on, that is more your responsibility than anyone else's.

So I decided, henceforth I will take on all remarks that come my way, the positive and the negative. I will analyse each one and take the helpful bits out of each one of them. Even the most negative remark will have some positivity embedded somewhere in what is being said or written, and that is what I will draw my attention to. It is then that I will truly improve in whatever I set my mind on doing. I have come to learn that decisions need to be made early on; we need to make the decision to continue to do what is right in our hearts no matter what negativities people may throw at us. Life is about diversity and we all cannot conform to the same methodologies, otherwise we will end up creating a wonderfully boring world.

My dream to one day stand before men and women and share my life experience with large audiences is still very much alive; when the time comes I will do my talking using lots of illustrative jokes to keep my audience interested; I will be informal and very relaxed. I will give my listeners hope and inspiration and they will love me for what I do. I have decided to keep on dreaming, especially as dreaming does not cost a lot. I have decided that I will listen to criticism only because I am not deaf but I will forge ahead and continue to do whatever it takes to make my dream become real.

It would be a good idea if you could make the same decision towards your dreams – decide to hold your head very high up and forge ahead despite any let downs no matter what form they might come in or who from.

3. That thing in your heart

Now that it is beginning to dawn on me that I am getting old really fast, I have been putting myself out on many development training programmes lately. It is never too late you see. Anyway, I was on one of such trainings during the week. This particular course runs for a whole year during which we have to attend a few workshops at regular intervals to review each module. I was the third person to arrive for the workshop on the day and I was quick to notice that the other two delegates had their 'suitcases' of books that we were given at the initial workshop. Oops! I thought – I did not bring mine because I was not told to, I didn't think I would need them and they were too much of a load anyway.

My fellow learners started coming in one by one each one holding their 'suit case'. I was praying fervently that at least one of them would come in without their books so that I wouldn't be the only loafer, however my wish never materialised. To make matters even more interesting everyone knew I was the only one without my books. By the time we finished the training many hours later – not one reference was made to the books, we simply did not have to bring them in the first place, which meant that I was right all along - hence it was now my turn to do the 'he who laughs last' thingy!

I was happy I did not call up any of my colleagues to ask if we had to bring the books prior to attending the class. I am sure they would have said yes, and they would have been wrong anyway. I am quite glad that I followed my heart.

I know, you know and even the rest of the world knows that good advice is priceless; however this is only relevant when you can get good advice. In many cases you either cannot find the appropriate person to counsel you; you could find it difficult to raise particular issues with anyone due to confidentiality, and many times previous experience prevents you from asking again, or maybe you just prefer that others do not know your business. There could be many factors that would rightly stop you from taking counsel from others, and many times you have to come to a verdict in isolation.

This is when the heart rules!

Ideally the verdict you make would need to be backed by appropriate actions otherwise you would have wasted the whole decision making process, especially as the refusal to take action could lead to creating a wider gap between where you are presently and where you think you should be – the bane of frustration.

There are times when we reach crossroads, times when there is a burning desire to get something done, a time when we need to do something in ways that may seem unconventional, times when we just want to get up and go. When these times are upon us, it is always best to just do those things that we know deep in our hearts are the right things to do.

The truth of the matter is that some of us ask for advice, not because we do not know what to do, but because we need some form of confirmation from someone else to do that which we would do anyway, so what exactly is the point? I mean if someone I had solicited some advice from had told me it's too soon to start on my third book do you think I would give them a second thought?

In many cases it is best to keep your ideas to yourself, nurture them, treat them like treasure and allow yourself and your God to develop your ideas in secret until the right time to expose them to the world comes, rather than telling someone who might unwittingly help you destroy your seed before the gestation period is done.

SEVEN

DETERMINATION

1. Building a castle – Contributed by Bola Iduoze

One lovely day, after playing away the best part of my first year in college, I got my result and for the first time in my life, the result was: Failed! Advised to withdraw! All of a sudden, the lovely day became a grey and dull day! All hope seemed lost and life seemed to have come to an unexpected end. Why should I go on? Will I ever pass again? Failure has come, the end has come, I thought.

As I have experienced, and many of us experience, failure, is a scary word. It is the bottom line on many of our fears. We fear failing as a spouse, what if I make a lousy husband or wife? What if I am a bad parent and my child turns out very bad due to my poor parenting skills? What if my business fails? What if my career leads me nowhere? These questions always come and they wreak havoc on our sense of peace.

It's amazing that for some people, failure is a stepping stone. Their failure makes them stronger and results in great things. For many, it's a millstone; they were cruising along, hit a divorce or a disease or a major disappointment, and then everything went downhill. The millstone goes around their neck and hangs there forever. What makes the difference?

The first thing to realise is that failure is universal, you are not the only one who has gone through it and you will not be the last to experience it. As long as you are a human being on planet Earth, I have news for you: failure and disappointments will come. The only issue is how you're going to deal with it. Where will you be when the wave is over and the storms have blown over? Will you be found still standing or totally blown over and not able to take any more daring steps in life?

The second thing to realize is that the fear of failure can be a dominating force in your life. The fear of failure is worse than the failure itself. Some people shy away from starting a business, getting into a relationship, or exploring their dreams and goals because they just might fail. They miss the marriage or the career they could have had-all because of fear.

What will you do with your dream or thought? Will you crumble in fear of failure or will you, with God's help and assistance give it all you've got?

The end of my story is, yes, I failed that year in college, but I learnt so much from it and it made me the better person I am today. There have been many other successes after that failure and many other joys following that disappointment.

Don't build a castle in the place of your former failure...it's time to move on!

2. Staying Alive

Lack of motivation!

This is one of the many factors that hinder people from running with their dreams. We sometimes stop to think 'what exactly is the point'. It takes grace to be self motivated; however every individual owes it to himself or herself to ensure that the desire to reach their ultimate goal remains constantly illuminated.

There are so many factors in life that seem to drag us down and inhibit us from wanting to take another step to our promised land. You could however train yourself to recognise what factors are hindering your motivation to go on for another day, and use the same factor(s) to your own advantage as a tool to enhance your progression.

One day a farmer's donkey fell down into a well. The animal cried piteously for hours as the farmer tried to figure out what to do. Finally he decided the animal was old, and the well needed to be covered up anyway; it just wasn't worth it to retrieve the donkey.

He invited all his neighbours to come over and help him. They each grabbed a shovel and began to shovel dirt into the well. At first, the donkey realized what was happening and cried horribly. Then, to everyone's amazement, he quieted down. A few shovel loads later, the farmer looked down the well and he was astonished at what he saw.

As every shovel of dirt hit his back, the donkey did something amazing. He would shake it off and take a step up. As the farmer's neighbours continued to shovel dirt on top of the animal, he would shake it off and take a step up. Pretty soon, everyone was amazed, as the donkey stepped up over the edge of the well and trotted off!

Life is going to shovel dirt on you, all kinds of dirt which could easily affect your motivation and easily want to change your direction at every turn. The trick to getting out of a hole is to shake it off and take a step up to ensure that your desire 'stays alive'. Each of our hindrances is a stepping stone. We can get out of the deepest holes just by not stopping, never giving up!

Shake off that obstacle and take a step up!

3. Stick to it

In order to fulfil your divine destiny, you have to know your purpose in life and stick to the plan of getting to your dreamland.

You need a plan and then you must work within that plan, and planning should ideally be a daily event. You should wake up each day knowing where you're going, which direction you will take to get there and what you want to accomplish. Once you find your purpose, stick with it! Don't allow the distractions of life to get you off course. Ask yourself, "Is what I'm doing moving me toward my God-given destiny? Am I staying focused? Is this my purpose or am I just wasting my time being busy?" Don't be distracted and spend your time, money and energy on things that may be interesting, but are not helping you fulfil your destiny. Unnecessary distractions will ultimately lead you to an unnecessary destination.

Remember, God's plans are blessed and as you walk in His plan for your life, you will experience His abundant blessing on everything you set your hand to do.

4. The law of average

I used to settle for average. I grew up accepting that reaching the average mark in anything I did was just good enough – but now I know better. God has planted His seed of hope, power and victory inside me! All I had to do actually was to allow God to bring the best out of my life and decide I wasn't going to settle for "good enough." Especially as I have come to realise that I need to press on toward the goal, unto the prize of the high calling of God in Christ Jesus (Philippians 3:14)

How about you?

It may not always be easy to do this, but it's very possible! Perhaps you have made a hurtful mistake in your past, (who hasn't?) that is still haunting you. If you let the enemy tell you that you're not good enough for God's forgiveness, then you're settling for less than God's victory. Setbacks are part of life, but Jesus said He came to give you an abundant life! If you decide to strive for excellence, there is no limit to what the Lord can do through you and with you – He is there to lend the most helpful helping hand

5. The passion; the anger; the frustration

A few years ago I discovered a very well known website where you could read various inspirational thoughts and stories. I usually visit the site at least once a week and feed myself with words of wisdom and encouragement. Earlier this year I decided to take a step further – rather than just read other peoples piece of writing and end my journey there, I came to a decision to put some of my own articles on the website for others to draw inspiration from. To do this, I had to click on a 'submit your document' button, get redirected to an email address where you send your document to. I have been doing this for a few months because I happen to be very passionate about using inspirational thoughts to inspire people, just as I get motivated by reading other peoples articles.

So that explains the Passion bit!

Now you are aware of the fact that I submit articles to a website; the other bit to my story that you might find a little interesting is that, none, zero, not even one of my many articles has been 'uploaded' onto the website. I check the site at least once a week to see if any of my stuff is there and each time I get disappointed and angry at not finding one of my many articles on the website; it simply does my head in.

And that explains the anger bit!

Now; can you think back a bit and answer the following question with all honesty, "What are you passionate about?" I mean what issues make your heart bubble. After a few minutes of thought you might come up with a few subjects on your list. Next question; of the many subject matters that you might have thought of, which one really gets your back up? Which of these issues has frustrated you in the past simply because you could not deal with the matter the way you would have loved to? Maybe, just maybe, you are destined to solve that 'problem'. Better put – your calling maybe in the solution to the problem that you are so passionate about, passionate enough to get you angry and frustrated. Do you know that some (actually most) of the worlds most fascinating inventions where born out of anger and frustration; and sometimes frustration is the best form of motivation. For instance only recently in the States, Glendale businessman Jack Fisher came up with an invention called the Easy Dump Trash Can after getting fed up one day while trying to bag his grass clippings. He had mowed his lawn and dumped the grass into a bag. The bag stretched when he tried to lift it out of the trashcan and the grass spilled onto the ground. Fisher kicked the metal trash can out of frustration. It landed upside down, and that's when Fisher saw the value of a can with a wider bottom and a narrower top. His invention currently sells in its millions.

So out of my frustration, I decided to rename and revamp my website. I have now created an avenue for as many that are interested to submit write ups that will serve as a tool of encouragement to others. The website is now a tool for which you (oh yea you) can share your thoughts with a very large World Wide Web enthusiasts.

It also means that I can now submit my write ups and I am rest assured that they will appear on my website at least.

Gosh! I am happy I got that of my chest!

So what are you passionate about, what exactly gets you gnashing your teeth because you feel a bit let down about it, and what do you desire so much that all you do is get frustrated? Maybe it's time you get up and do something about it!

EIGHT

ENCOURAGEMENT

1. Go on; be one of the very few

We can pretend as much as we want to, but we all love to be appreciated. Okay, we might tend to put on a macho outward show, but when searched inward enough, everyone wants to be appreciated for what he / she has done, or achieved.

If you agree with the above, then I guess you might as well believe that the man (or woman) who you see from afar might also want to be acknowledged.

I have learnt from experience (unfortunately) that it is not how hard you work, or how much extra time that you put into whatever you do that gets you noticed or appreciated. It is not the fact that you hardly 'throw a sicky' that gets you promoted. Being the best dressed in the office might get you noticed but not a lot more.

No matter what you want to achieve in life – you will have to go through people to get to your dreamland. Some of the people you require to aid you get to the next level come across your path in different ways and forms; and what do you do when you get to stumble upon such people? You do what everyone else does, the norm. For instance, if you attend a seminar where your company director is giving a fantastic presentation, what do you do once the presentation is over? – clap just like everyone else.

o   If you work very hard; there is someone who works harder, so how do you stand out?

- o   If you hardly take time off sick, there are many who fall into the same category!

- o   If you always submit your report on time; I'm sure you are not the only one that does this!

- o   If you are always there for your Pastor to call on; surely there are few others like you!

- o   Just because your shop opens early and closes late will not necessarily attract the high number of customers that you crave for.

- o   Never late to anything? Trust me you are not alone.

So how do you stand out; how do you get noticed. What will give you the recognition that will get you the attention of someone who may be able to make the difference in your life?

Statistically, out of every 100 delegates to any particular seminar (or presentation); only one, yeah just on delegate goes to the presenter to tell them how well the presentation went! That one that will definitely get noticed!

If the head of cooperation sends out a 'notice of increment in pay' email to all 500 of the workforce, just five will send back an email to the head to say 'thank you'. The other 495 staff will think it's their birth right!

Zig Ziglar wrote; "you can get everything in life you want if you'll just help enough other people get what they want".

And what is it that we all want, no matter who we are, what we do, or even if we pretend that we do not want it, that thing is "Appreciation / Acknowledgement".

Why don't you genuinely appreciate and acknowledge someone; make a conscious effort to let someone know that they have done well. Once this becomes part of your 'being', just watch as more people will love you, and that man or woman will recognise you enough to assist you in getting to the next level.

Only about 1% of any group of people do this; Go on; be one of the very few!

In the book of Luke 17:19, the only leper that came back to show his appreciation to Christ was made 'whole'. The others, oh well.............................

2. My friend; JUMP

I was about 16 I think, it was a very hot afternoon in the good city of Lagos; it was after my GCSE O'Level examinations on my way home from a friend's crib.

I was in a situation.

From where I was standing I could see the bus stop I needed to get to, but there was a massive 'gutter' between me and the bus stop. About ½ a mile away there was a footbridge. I could always do the sensible thing and walk ½ a mile, walk across the footbridge and walk another ½ a mile back to the bus stop. Taking this option was the sensible choice – but it will come at a price. By the time I walked to the bus stop I would be 17 and very tired. More significantly, I could easily miss the bus anyway.

The other option was to jump over the gutter and I would be at the bus stop five minutes later. This way I would have saved a whole lot of time, saved so much energy, definitely caught my bus and I would still be 16. However; there was a risk here. You see this gutter was no ordinary gutter. The 'stuff' running in the gutter was pure sewage. The smell alone could kill anyone who hangs around it for too long – imagine what would happen if I fell into it. The greatest worry was that if I fell into the trench no one would be willing to get in to rescue me. Even if I was able to drag myself out of the mess, what bus driver would be willing to give me a ride home? This will mean that I would have had to walk home – about 15 miles away stinking really badly. Many would easily pass me for a mad man or some destitute.

Anyway, back to my predicament. I stood at the edge of the gutter accessing my success ratio of jumping over the gutter. After a few minutes, I shook my handsome head and I was about to start my ½ a mile walk to the footbridge. As I turned around I heard a voice say – 'oh boy you can do it – my friend jump'. I looked into the guys' eyes, took a few backward steps, ran towards the gutter and took a giant leap.

I did it!

The guy who 'pushed' me smiled and said in Pidgin English 'I no tell you' (didn't I tell you) and he walked away from my life forever.

He saved my time, effort, energy and a whole lot of stench.

Sometimes we all find ourselves in situations where we think that it is simply impossible to deal with certain circumstances. What we tend to do is try to deal with the issues ourselves and we very often come out at the other end with a massive stench. There are few methods that can be employed to save us time, money, effort and energy.

One of them is a good PUSH! However, this is only available for those who are willing to be PUSHED!

3. Now I know – contributed by Bola Iduoze

Apparently, 'experience is the best teacher', although I've also heard one or two people say, even though experience is the best teacher, its school fees are very expensive, so it's better to let someone else experience it than yourself.

Many of us go through tough situations and tough times, but the main problem is that we do not look for the lessons to be learnt within the tough times, so when the tough time is over, and relief comes, we just cannot wait to forget how tough the times were and cannot wait to move on. The challenge however comes when we go through a similar experience again, and we then seem to be going around in circles.

Every challenge has a seed of advantage, or something to learn from it, only if we take time out to look closely and learn from them. In every defeat is a lesson of how to win the victory next time. Again, that can only be learnt if we examine the defeat, look closely at why we were defeated and see what we can learn from the situation and what to do differently if you ever come across such situation again.

There will be things that will come your way that will seem like adversities or problems, take time to examine them closely, as there will be something to learn that will bring victory your way!

4. So what should I do?

I was at a ceremony recently when one of those who took to the stage asked me how he his performance went.

Oh; fantastic I responded.

Another friend standing by said that it would not matter if the performance was good, average or even poor, Ayodele (that's me) would always give a positive comment. He went on to say that my ideology of giving positive comments all the time could be deceptive because I could be sending the wrong impression to the person involved. According to my good friend, the message I was giving out was deceptive and could lead to false assurance in the person the message is being relayed to. I need to be bold enough to tell 'whom it may concern' the reality of the situation. I should be able to tell them that their performance was bad, if it is and give positive feedbacks when I genuinely believe that the person had done a good job.

I guess he was right!

The comments got me thinking all week. I had to reassess myself in relation to how I give feed backs to people; I re-examined my 'assertiveness' in dishing out words that could be perceived as deceptive and hence lead to false self believe in those that I come in contact with. I 'almost' concluded that henceforth I was going to change my approach and tell people as it is. If they had performed badly, I will put it to them in very firm terms that they had goofed and massive improvements have to be made for them to get anywhere – I am going to get tough.

I pondered over this for the entirety of the week, and during my tinkering, I remembered so very much some comments that had put me in the red in the past. I remember a one time manager of mine who once gave me an 'honest opinion' of a piece of work I had done. Her comments were so honest that I almost gave up on my career because I thought I was not good enough. I remembered how I felt when a friend once told me that I will not be able to speak publicly because of my accent. I also remembered how I felt when at a very tender age a teacher told me that I was the dullest student he had ever met. Then, I got to realise that I must be unique. There cannot be too many people out there who only see the good in what people do. I strongly believe that most people give 'constructive' (maybe destructive) criticism and I really do not need to join the bandwagon because my friend said so. More so, if almost everyone else gives not very reassuring comments, this will equally mean that very few people get positive comments in anything they do.

So I came to my final decision. I will remain that encouraging voice for the rest of my life; and this how it will work:

When Joe Bloggs embarks on an activity which might require feedback, I know that most people will be 'constructive' enough in their comments to him. When it is my turn to say something, I will look at the 'tiny good' in what might have been a 'poor' performance and tell him what they are. This will hopefully be a something for Mr Bloggs to hold and give him hope that he could do better.

In conclusion, I want to remain the way I am; I like it!

5. Sun is shinning – contributed by Folakemi Togunloju

I have always wondered what it was about summer that made people automatically appear happy.

I associate summer with colourful clothes, being out until late on a weekday because it's so bright, lots of people on the streets, lots of people smiling.

Is there some sort of chemical in the atmosphere that automatically alters our thinking? Why can we not be like that during the cold dark winter months? In January whilst I was still working out of London, I used to wear my customary Black long jacket but over it I used to wear a bright (very bright) orange scarf (I got strange looks on the train). On getting to work one day, a colleague commented "that's really bright", to which I said; it's my little sunshine on surviving the dark depressing days of leaving and returning home when it's dark. I worked in a corporate environment where everyone thought it necessary to only wear black. Imagine how depressing that can look even when you are having a good day. And then you picture a black girl in black wearing a bright orange scarf, it always made me smile when I saw my reflection through the windows.

That scarf was my symbol of "I don't care how dark it gets, and how black everyone looks, I want something that would put that summer feeling into my brain".

Sometimes we need to create that little something, that when we look at, regardless of what it is, just puts a smile on your face and lifts your spirit. I used to have a picture of my lovely and adorable niece as my background on my computer at work. Every time I switched on my computer, I always smiled (I became an aunty for the first time because of her). So imagine how many times that help, you come back from a frustrating meeting and the first thing you see is this innocent baby smiling at you. Picture that. I tend to have road rages in my car when I drive and along with the air freshener in my car is a picture of my niece hanging there to make me smile when I am getting edgy because of the traffic or someone cutting in front of me. For now these little quirky things work. Maybe I'll change them in the future to something else, maybe a picture of my own daughter. But for now, it's refreshing to enter my car and smile every time I look at the picture.

When it becomes difficult to smile or lift yourself up, grabbing hold of something regardless of what it is that makes your spirit lighter could make a world of difference. It could be a picture of your kids, spouse, shinning new car, a bright scarf, anything that ensures the sun keeps shinning in your life.

NINE

FEAR

---

1. Be afraid; be very afraid

There you are, wanting to do something tangible for yourself. You have been putting off taking the initial steps that will lead you to achieving that dream which until now has only remained a dream. Maybe one of the reasons why you have been putting the process off is because you have been afraid. You have spent time worrying about the consequences of failure, the consequences of becoming an object of ridicule, the consequences of losing your investment and maybe the consequences of losing your dignity.

You ponder forever on whether you are about to do the right thing and you get apprehensive and very much afraid.

I guess you have been told a few times that fear is from the devil and you should not be afraid and all the blah, blah, and blah that goes with such talk. Some people must have told you that you should not be afraid but you must be courageous and eliminate fear from your life; yeah right! – Like it's that easy.

Everyone is fearful from time to time – what really matters is the distinguishing between 'good fear' and 'bad fear' and then knowing how to convert your bad fear into good fear.

Bad fear cripples and inhibits. It slows you down by reminding you that the step you are about to take is a bit too much for you and you are very likely to soon become a 'joke' if you dare pursue your dream. When bad fear resides inside you, nobody needs to tell you that you are small; you will tell yourself this everyday anyway. Bad fear makes you concentrate on the potential loses you may encounter in trying to take the magical step, rather than concentrating on the potential gains. Bad fear – horrible thing!!!

On the other hand good fear, even though it is still referred to as fear has a different type of hold on you. The good fear acts as a propellant that thrusts you forward although your knees might be seriously knocking against each other while you are in flight. Good fear makes you concentrate on what you will lose if you do not take the step of faith rather than focusing on what will happen to you if you fail to achieve your goal.

In a nutshell, your fears are your fears and no matter what the motivational speaker tells you, by the time you finish listening to him/her you will still be fearful. This is where your willpower needs to take pre-eminence. It is down to you to decide if your fear is a good fear or otherwise.

I was working for the railways for a while; actually I think I stayed with the organisation for over seven years. During this period I always had my hand up to indicate that I wanted to progress within the organisation. My request was ignored over and over again until it became a bit of a bother. I eventually got a little upward movement only to get stuck again. It became apparent to me that it was time to move on; it was time for me to look for another job outside the railways before I got too old for employment elsewhere. But there was something holding me back from trying – yeah you guessed right; Fear. I was scared of leaving the job that I was very much used to for something that may well be outside my comfort zone. I was fearful of the land of the unknown. I feared that my limited skills will make me a laughing stock in the corporate world. To make matters even worse, the jobs available to me at the time were temporary contract jobs. I was going to leave a permanent job where I had all the rights under the sun for, a job were I could be kicked out for sneezing too loud. I had bad fear holding me down.

I had to make a decision – I had deal with my fear by turning it from bad fear to good fear.

I was still very much fearful, but the difference was that this time around I was fearful of the consequences of not making the move when I had the opportunity to. I decided to fear the consequences of continuing to earn embarrassing wages for a very long time, until a time when I will be left with no choice but to continue hanging on to a hopeless job. I feared regretting my lacklustre attitude many years later. I feared that sometime soon I might struggle to pay my mortgage if the pace at which interest rates are going up was anything to go by. I feared continuing being the tea boy even at the age of forty.

I was afraid, very afraid – so afraid that I had to act; my fear propelled me into changing my job.

So please be afraid, there is nothing wrong with being afraid – but be sure it is the good fear.

2. Nice Dress

I was getting ready to go out to a party with my wife the other day. She asked me what I was going to wear and I told her I was going to pick something out of the wardrobe; it was already ironed and ready to be worn. "Shame", she said. "I was going to ask you to iron mine for me". "That's not a problem, just tell me where your outfit is and I will get it ironed for you", I responded. She pointed to a bag under her dressing table and I got the dress out. I looked at it for a while, and I told her how nice I thought the dress was. "It must have cost you a lot of money", I remarked. "Actually, it didn't cost a lot; my cousin did the tailoring for me at no cost", she responded. I paused for a few minutes, looked at the dress and then I asked my wife which of the cousins made the dress. Even after telling me who the cousin was over and over again I still found it difficult to believe that the dress was not made by an expensive designer with a mega studio somewhere in the heart of London.

My wife had had enough of my disbelieve; so she called her cousin, gave me the phone and asked me to talk to her.

The cousin confirmed that she made the dress. She never charges for her services because she had no formal training in the profession – she just picked up a 'hobby' in sewing.

Hobby!

I asked why she has not considered going professional and make some money by putting her God given skill to full use. Her response, "I have thought about it a few times, but I am a bit scared of embarking on tailoring full time.

The stronghold called Fear!

Do you think Tiger Woods would have been a bit more satisfied with life if he was an IT consultant somewhere and his golfing skills were just a hobby? I wonder what would have become of David Beckham if his football skills were just a hobby. The world would have missed out on the brilliant 'One Love' if Bob Marley had been afraid to break out of the trench where he grew up, and instead sang with his ghetto brethren at football matches. When Will Smith was repeatedly told he had the gift of making people laugh, he could have taken the comments as mere compliments and 'hobbilised' his gift. Instead, he helped save the world from the visitors from space on the American Independence day.

The bane of the 'nine to five'!

So many of us are bound to our 'today money' that we fail to as much as try out the free Gift that God has given us to make us stand out and make a difference. We get up every morning and step out to work, come back flat out and left with no energy to as much as think of putting our talents to use. There will always be conflicts between what we term as hobbies and what we class gifts and talents. The force that prevents many of us from differentiating between the two is fear. When fear prevents you from expressing your gift, the gift gets relabelled as a hobby. When I tell some of the members of the choir of my local church that they have what it takes to become real stars in the music world, they shrug their shoulders in a manner that says – it's just a hobby. Deep down, the real reason why they give me the shrug is because they earn enough from what they do in their nine to five; why would they want to rock the boat? They are more than happy to ask the congregation to raise their hands and wave to the Lord. I think in addition to that, they should be asking themselves to raise their own hands and find out how best they could turn their hobbies into rewarding careers – otherwise called Gifts and Talents.

Back to my wife's cousin; I told her to start small. Rather than sew beautiful dresses for free, she should ask for payment for services rendered. She should print complementary cards/fliers and hand them out to friends, colleagues and members of her family. She would soon be so occupied with sewing, making money and becoming famous that she would have to leave her nine to five and turn a hobby into the life changing gift it is.

I know my wife would be more than willing to support her cousin – all the cousin needs to do is believe.

It's high time some of us shook off the stronghold of fear and at least start small.

TEN

FOCUS

---

1. And there was Peter – contributed by DJ Sobanjo

I was actually brooding on this subject of FOCUS on the way in to work and I was reflecting on my personal experiences as well as the wisdom I have gleaned from both my direct mentors and my virtual mentors.

And I have come to conclude that focusing on challenges is one of the top reasons why many people never achieve their dreams.

Don't get me wrong I'm not saying you are not going to face any challenges. Oh my goodness, you most definitely are, if you're not facing challenges, it means you are not doing anything significant. Rather, what I'm saying is if you focus on your challenges, your challenges are magnified making them seem bigger than they really are.

This could drain your energy and cause you to doubt the ability of your God and lose sight of your dreams.

Let me tell you a personal story, maybe this would help you understand what I'm trying to show you. Among other things I build a marketing business from home working with a huge manufacturer of lifestyle enhancing products. This business has been a real blessing for us. Things were actually going quite well for us; we had made some good money.

There was a particular period around December last year where I decided to sit down and 'review' my business. I was looking out for the customers who had been with us the year before who were no longer with us. We had lost quite a number of customers. I started to feel depressed. I was really upset. The more I focused on what we had lost, the less active I became. Our productivity level dropped and for 3 months we did absolutely nothing to move that business forward. This is really amazing because in that same period I decided to focus on the challenges we were facing which was business retention. I had disregarded the fact that our business had more than doubled in size in that same period and also we had been recognised as having one of the top 5 growing businesses in Europe with the company we had partnered with.

I chose to focus on the challenges and almost destroyed what we had built because of that.

Also, there's the story in the Bible of a gentleman called Peter. It was a stormy night and he was out at sea in a boat with his friends, then he saw Jesus approaching the boat walking on water, He called out and Jesus asked him to come over. Peter stepped out of the boat and as he focused on Jesus, he found himself walking on water towards Him.

Then suddenly Peter, looked around him, noticed the heavy winds, the great waves and the thunderous rains and was overwhelmed by these great challenges and immediately he began to drown. Thankfully Jesus was there to guide in on.

2. Evoking shouts of joy

You have a great dream and a vision for your life. Everyone does; that's what keeps people motivated during the tough times.

When times get a bit harder than expected, you need to remind yourself that "there will be shouts of joy when the world hears of your victory, flags flying with praise to God for all that He has done for you" (Psalm 20:5).

The problem isn't that some people forget to have dreams, the worry however is that we sometimes don't do our part to fulfil those dreams and we allow them to come to pass. God wants us to pursue and fulfil our dreams, and not to let everyday life stand in the way.

There are many daily routines to be done such as your nine to five and watching TV but don't let these things stop you from striving towards the goals God has put in your heart. He doesn't want you to stop until you have discovered all that He has in store for you!

To evoke shouts of joy in heaven and in earth, you will need to stay focused.

3. It's around the corner

It is a real shame that as we grow up we tend to sometimes loose some of the will power we had when we were kids.

The power of the young!

As kids we usually have dreams and aspirations of what we want to do or become and the desire is generally so strong that it takes a lot to kill such dreams. The will to get things done seems to get thinner as we grow older. The will power I see in my daughters sometimes reminds me how determined I was to get the little things done when I was a teenager and how different forms of distractions unfortunately killed some of the will power I once had.

I was about 9 years old in a mixed boarding school somewhere in the rural part of Nigeria. My dad would pop in to see me and my sister every fortnight and usually bring us some provisions and money. One particular weekend I was desperate for a visit from my dad because we were asked to buy a particular book and this had to be shown to the teacher first thing on the following Monday morning. Any student who failed to bring the book to class by the set deadline would get some form of punishment. So I was desperate.

Saturday came and there was no sight of my dad, Sunday morning dawned and no show. At midday I was getting increasingly worried. By the evening I decided to take drastic action.

I made sure no one was watching and then I sneaked through the gates of the school compound and started a long walk.

Walk to where?

I knew that my grandparents lived in some village down the road from school and I knew they would buy me the book if I could get to them. When my dad takes me to see his parents in his car, it usually seemed like a short distance. How wrong!

So there I was, a kid with a tiny body frame and extra skinny legs, walking alone down a very lonely road and it was beginning to get dark. After about 30 minutes I began to tell myself that I would get there because it is just around the corner. It began to get darker and the cars that drove past had their head lamps on but no one bothered to stop to offer me a ride; that was understandable though – I could have been a young ghost! Anyway I continued my trek for another 30 minutes and came to a familiar roundabout, wow; the village should be around the corner I thought to myself. I walked pass the roundabout and even after a further 30 minutes walk the village was no where in site. At this time it was pitch black and I could hardly see (what streetlights?). I knew I could not turn back, I just had to continue. I was certain that the route was the same that my dad takes to get to the village; I had only underestimated the distance a little bit. I was getting scared, very scared but I had to forge ahead. I had reached a point of no return. Various thoughts were running riot in my head such as the possibility of a 'monster' jumping out of the nearby bushes and cutting off my little head.

After about 3½ hours or strenuous walking I got to the village, a further 20 minutes and I got to my grandparents house. I walked in, and the first person I met was my dads' sister. She was shocked to see me and asked me how I got to the village from school; 'I walked!'

I was later told that she fainted when I told her this; I did not see her faint because apparently I fainted first. I woke up the next day with two legs that seemed heavier that I left them the night before. I went back to school the next day (in a car) to face some severe punishment for my efforts; but at least I had my book in my hand.

Now that I'm older I seem to have lost some of that drive. The drive to keep on going, especially when the Promised Land seems a bit far! But you know what, anytime I think of the above incident, it reminds me to keep on going. What do you think?

4. Looking away – Contributed by Kolade Ayodele

Quite truly, distractions represent hindrances to success and often break or disrupt momentum. Will be sure to be laser focused constantly and also snap back on track when distracted.

5. Looking where?

One of the greatest to hindrances to progress is the inability to take our eyes off the past. Taking eyes off the past includes disallowing previous failures from preventing you from looking ahead and allowing previous successes to blindfold you from seeing a greater future.

You may be hurting and aching from your past, but take heart, for God is with you! God wants to help you recover these things, as well as the lost years of blessings as written in Isaiah 43:18 "Forget the former things; do not dwell on the past". In fact, His desire is to give them back to you in even greater abundance. No matter where you are today, no matter where you've been in the past, God wants to give you a new future filled with joy, fulfilment and abundance. God's power will help you break the chains of your past so you can face tomorrow anticipating His blessing and favour. Look ahead to the blessings He has for you, not back to any hurt or suffering that may be in the past. So if you're looking back today, turn around and start looking ahead.

6. On the journey! – contributed by Olamide Sanni

It's so sad when inspite of seemingly infallible planning, failure culminates.

As we journey through life, we are faced with hindrances, impediments, constraints and stumbling blocks. So many times, we fall flat on our faces! Whilst keeping an eye on our desired destination, the focus should be on the journey itself. To lead a purpose filled life, we must remember that we will remain on course throughout the journey if we are able to stand, as the problems that we face are a part of the journey.

We must remember that we do not fail by getting knocked down; we fail by staying down...

7. One big road with lot a of signs

I left work one day during the week, drove to the nursery school to pick up our youngest daughter. From the moment I set my eyes on her I knew she was tired and I could tell it was going to be a bit of a troublesome drive home. I got her into her car seat and once I started the 10 minutes drive home she started throwing a tantrum as she usually does whenever she is tired. I did everything I could to calm her down including threatening to throw her out of my car. Anyway, she soon calmed down and for some strange reason she went very quiet – peace at last I thought. Suddenly she said something rather very profound, "I love you daddy, but I want my mummy". I burst into uncontrollable laughter feeling proud of my young lady who loved me but knew exactly what she wanted, and at that moment it wasn't me.

One of the keys to living a truly successful life is by keeping your focus.

It is one thing to know exactly what we want at different stages of our life, it is an entirely different matter when it comes to keeping our eyes on that which matters most. The challenge remains the competition.

There are always many competitors struggling to get our attention, and these contestants come in various forms and sizes. They are usually very attractive or extremely ugly and they tend to descend upon us at the most vulnerable times. They tend to want to shift our concentration from the issues that really matter and then leave us dealing with the things that would have been better left alone. These unwanted competitors are usually short lived, but their effects are usually very much long termed, leaving behind legacies of regrets and failures. They are very powerful, powerful enough to want to make you detour from your well laid plan. Imagine what would have happened if Jesus had drifted away from His purpose by agreeing to be made a king on earth.

The effect of losing focus results in the inability to see the start and the end of short or long term projects especially. The vision that has been put into our hearts becomes a bit blurry and overcast because other concerns have taken the place of such visions in our life. So you set out to own your own home, suddenly your landlord for some strange reason, offers to improve the estate making it a bit more attractive to live in which leads to the death of your drive to want to get on the property ladder. You are just about to commence putting things in place to start up that business you have always longed for, and then you suddenly get promoted, hence more responsibility at work leading to a blurred focus in relation to your dream business.

Keeping an eye on what matters the most.

We live a very busy life with many issues and situations fighting constantly for our attention and we are always surrounded by the attractions that come with life. There is a need to differentiate between the needed and the wanted, between the things that have to be done imminently and those things that can wait another day, the difference between what we need to add to ourselves and what constitutes extra baggage, the difference between the relationships we need to nurture and those that we need to shake off – its all about focusing on what matters the most.

It is very easy to go through a circle in life; a circle of 'I have been here before'. This is a circle in which we keep on dreaming about a particular feat, and because we feel a sense of emptiness without the realisation of our dream we keep on revisiting the dream in our head. The problem is that it will only remain a dream until we resolve to give the desire our full attention. Until we learn to fight off the many contenders for our attention and stick to what will make a difference in our life, we will continue to be dreamers and not achievers.

Life is like a big road with loads of signs trying to tell us which way to go. Decide on the sign you want to follow and drive carefully to your place of fulfilment.

8. Opps! I am going the wrong way

As part of my fatherly duties I drop my younger girl at her nursery school on my way to work and then pick both girls up from their respective playgroups on my way back. If I have to start work late, which I must say happens once in a blue moon, I drop off both girls on my way to work. I also take both girls to school anytime I am off from work. The long and short of this is that I rarely take my older girl to school.

Last week my older daughter was going away for three days to on a school trip. On the day she was leaving for the trip I went to her room, prayed for her and kissed her goodbye. I grabbed the younger one and off we went on our very familiar trip. I was driving along ignoring the little person in the back seat and thinking of how much I was going to miss her sister; then suddenly I realised that I was going the wrong way. I was driving towards my elder daughters' school. Silly me; I had to turn back and start my journey all over again.

Does this sound familiar to you? – Maybe not! Have you ever thought of doing something significant for yourself and then end up doing something entirely different? Have you ever set your mind on accomplishing a task and find yourself never getting to the end of it?

My journey the other day made me realise how the mechanism of the mind works. When you set your mind on getting something done, all you need to do is allow the influence of distractions take over; then watch as failure sets in.

It is a matter of the mind. Simply put, what you think of the most will manifest sooner or later. If you set your mind on being successful in a particular aspect of your life, if you blank out any thought of failure, if you free yourself of any negative hindrances even when they gaze you in the face, if you occupy your mind with the goodness of what you are trying to achieve; then success is guaranteed.

What is the point hoping for success and thinking failure?

Everyday of your life, continue to 'think' yourself as the best in whatever you are currently doing – and with time you will be the best

'Think' yourself as living out your dreams – no one will be able to hinder your progress

'Think' your children growing up to become the envy of the world – and they will grow up to be children that you will forever be proud of.

'Think' yourself as being source of joy and happiness to people – you will become a people magnet.

'Think' yourself as the most charismatic person living – you will be loved by many.

'Think' yourself as a failure – oh well, I cannot really help you here!

But remember that according to Proverbs 23: 7 - for as he (a man) thinks in his heart, so is he (or so will he become).

9. People Matter

I need to make a confession – I have an addiction.

It's a very chronic addiction that I have been struggling with for most of my life. It has been with me from the young age of about ten, and thirty years later, the addiction is only getting stronger and stronger.

I would have asked for help a long time ago, but there is a problem – I like the addiction and I really do not want to give it up.

I am sure you want to know what my addiction is – shamefully I confess; I am addicted to Coke. No not that one; I mean Coca Cola. Give me coke, and you give me happiness!

Now that I have got that off my chest – I need to tell you something about the company that produces my favourite drink.

A very long time ago, Coca Cola was the best selling beverage in America (and the rest of the world, but for this write up I want to concentrate on the Americans). Suddenly, the sales of Coca Cola went down and Pepsi took over. Pepsi soon became the number one selling beverage and the guys at the Coke house become very worried. They did everything they could think of to get back to the number one spot, but nothing worked. They employed marketing gurus and asked them to raise their advertising game so that my favourite drink would do better than Pepsi; but it never worked. Eventually, someone who had his head screwed on properly made a simple suggestion. He asked for some statistics and he found out that most Americans wanted a drink. All they wanted to do was quench their thirst and the brand was least of their concerns. So continuing with his thought, he concluded that the company had been focusing on the wrong thing. They have been spending a fortune focusing on the competition from a rival company, instead of focusing on what really mattered – the people.

Once the company realised their mistake, they stopped the rivalry with Pepsi, and instead they decided to help the people of America solve the problem of thirst.

How would they accomplish this?

Easy; where do the people really feel the full force of thirst? Places where they cannot easily come in touch with water or any other drink for that matter; places like train stations, sports grounds, and shopping centers. So Coca Cola decided to help these poor (not in terms of money) people by providing Coca Cola vending machines at the above named places. So, when Mr. Jones is taking his family out on a day trip, he gets to a train station feeling tired and thirsty. The kids need to kill their thirst as well; so what does Mr. Jones do? He goes to the vending machine provided by the nice people from Coca Cola and gets himself and his family my favourite drink.

Within months, the sales of Coca Cola went up, it went so high up that Pepsi could not, has not, and might never catch up – not as long as I continue to drink Coca Cola.

Many of us have the wrong foundation in terms of what we focus on. Our focus is on making money, becoming famous, having large ministries, becoming company executives and we lose focus on what really matters – People.

If we can spare a moment in our busy schedule and put people first in our thoughts and deliberations, our focus will change, and we will become people magnets.

People magnets solve people problems; people problem solvers are true achievers.

Everyday is a good day to refocus our attention on what matters. Changing our focus to solving people problems will make a difference to someone's life, and that is what the essence of our existence is really all about; solving people's problems.

10. Wake up and live

God wants to give us great and mighty things; He really does.

He wants to unleash the blessings of heaven right into our lap. But there is a condition that has to be met. God wants us to work and fight for them, because only then are they desires of our heart.

Unfortunately, sometimes we pass up blessings because of a lack of commitment and faith. Don't be one of these people, we dig in our heels, stand our ground, and fight the good fight of the one that wants to excel!

I have decided to stay focused and be ready to step up to what God has called me to do – do you want to join me?

Whatever your step of faith needs to be, take it today. Don't wait until everything is perfect. God wants better things for you in every area, but He wants to know that you desire these things as well.

He's ready to fight for you, so you know your effort won't be in vain

ELEVEN

FORGIVENESS

---

1. Set yourself free – contributed by Bola Iduoze

I read an interesting quote, here it is….

'Bitterness is like taking poison expecting that someone else would die from the effect.'

Just a quick word, if you are bitter about anything, let it go! It does you more harm than the other party whom you think has caused the bitterness.

Forgive and set yourself and them free; or better still – set yourself free!

2. Thank you for coming back

I grew up in a society which strongly believes in what is written in Proverbs 13:24 - "He who spares the rod hates his son, but he who loves him is careful to discipline him".

I was very young and in a boarding school which meant that I got to see my parents once a month if I was lucky. On one of his visits to see me and my sisters, my dad came with an aunty and after a few hours of catching up and the hugs and kisses that came with it, the time came for my dad to leave. This was usually a time of sorrow and happiness. Sorrow because I knew I might not see my favourite man for a few weeks and happiness because I knew he would usually give me my pocket money before he went. He dipped his hand into his pocket and handed me a currency note and I knew instantly that the money he gave me would not last a week, even if I tried hard to stretch it. So, what did I do? I flipped and threw a massive tantrum. I jumped up and down like a raving lunatic and shredded the note beyond recognition. My dad ignoring my act of psychosis, walked gently towards his car with my aunty, they got in, he started the engine and off they went. But l can only think that my dad had underestimated the determination of a 'child scorned'. I ran after his car and jumped right in front of it with no care of what might happen to the skinny legs that I had. He had to stop, he was not going to run over his only son, but it was obvious that he was upset by my actions. He was so mad that he could have killed me provided someone could assure him that he would not be imprisoned afterwards. Anyway he gave me 'the look' and drove off.

What I did not realise was that every other student was gathered in front of the hostel watching the spectacle that was going on. I shamefully walked back to the hostel thinking to myself 'I am a dead boy'. True to my speculation, as soon I walked into the hostel, the matron called me to her office, and introduced me to a cane which was much taller than I was. She told me in no uncertain terms that she was going to beat the living day light out of me for my act of lunacy. I had never been so scared in my whole life – I stood there feeling very vulnerable and helpless. No one was going to save me – not even the angels were going to rescue me from the wrath of the rather scary woman with a screwed up face standing in front of me. I gave up any hope of mercy and waited for the cane to inflict some throbbing on my poor body, aided by 'Miss Happy'.

I had given up any hope of being redeemed and then suddenly there was voice behind me saying "that's ok, I will deal with this my own way" – it was Daddy!

I jumped on him like I had never jumped before – "Thank you dad for coming back to forgive me and save me from Miss Happy" I uttered these words with tears in my beautiful eyes.

My dad told me that what I did was not very nice, he told me that he will not be giving me any more money as a form of punishment for my sins; he kissed me and promised to see me the following weekend – what a relief. He finally went back to the matron and told her clearly, "do not touch my son, I have dealt with the situation myself" – "You tell her daddy"!

For as long you live on this wonderful place called earth, people would offend you, and people that are closer to you will tend to offend you the most. Many times we hear about forgiving people so that our own sins can be forgiven – a theory otherwise called selfishness; we hear about forgiving people so that we could set those that offend us free from our hearts, hence experience freedom – a phenomenon better described as self-centeredness; we sometimes forgive those that offend us so that we can experience some sort of self satisfaction – a term better referred to as Me! Me!! Me!!!

True forgiveness is achieved when you do it because you love who ever had offended so much so that you do not want to see them loose their way because of what they might have done wrong. You reach the height of real forgiveness when you forgive because the relationship has to be mended so that you can continue to positively influence the offender's life. You truly forgive when you know that there is still more to do in the other person's life and you need to break down any barrier that may prevent this from happening.

You forgive to save the offender from the wrath of Miss Happy!

You truly forgive when it's all about the offender and not about what you might gain by being forgiving.

TWELVE

GRATITUDE

---

1. All is well – contributed by Oluwayomi Ojo

Contentment grows up from a grateful heart.

We may sometimes think to ourselves that we would be happy, if only......

However, some of the most discontented people are those who seem to have it all.

Contentment begins, not in having that one more thing that eludes our grasp, but in becoming deeply thankful for the things that are already within our grasp.

I have learned to be content with whatever I have. I know what it is to have little, and I know what to have plenty is. In any and all circumstances I have learned the secret of being well fed and of going hungry, of having plenty and of being in need.

I guess this explains why I love the song by Horatio G Spafford.

"When a peace like a river attends my way, when sorrow like sea billows roll, whatever my lot, Thou has taught me to say" It is well, it is well with my SOUL"

2. I had to go back

Many of us are born with, or develop confidence as we get older. I happen not to be one of those many. Confidence was never part of the attributes that I was endowed with and developing confidence has never been something that I was able to achieve for a long time either. Up until my early twenties, I struggled with my confidence and my degree of shyness was fast becoming an embarrassment.

While I was at the Polytechnic I was particularly reticent and I think the only person that knew my name in a class of over fifty, was me. I would creep in for lectures and creep back home.

Friends? What were they?

I was in my second year and we had just finished a lecture. I was standing among about 50 other students when I heard a voice calling my name. To make matters more worrying, the voice belonged to lady. I knew I was the only one with my surname but it never occurred to me that some lady would be shouting my name out loud, and things became even more interesting when I realised that the person calling me was one of the most highly respected female lecturers in the college. I kept wondering what on earth she wanted from me, but I was even more concerned about how on earth she knew my name.

Anyway, I eventually got myself to her office, and all she wanted to know was if I was coping well with my studies. She was genuinely interested in me and my well being that I suddenly felt a sense of care and love around me. I left her office after about twenty minutes feeling good about myself. For the remaining three years of my stay at the college, Mrs Adelawo would occasionally ask me how I was doing and this worked a treat for me. I really felt that someone really cared about me and I was able to grow in confidence, make friends and eventually come out of my shell.

I had completed my final exams and I decided to take a walk around the campus for the last time before I moved out of my room the next day. I did this with a friend who had also benefited from the good natured Mrs Adelawo. We both decided to pay this lovely lady one last visit, the only problem was that even though we knew she lived on campus, we had no idea where exactly. We eventually found out where she lived and we knocked on her door. She was shocked to say the least. We were invited in and we all had an hours worth of talking and going down memory lane. When we were about to leave, me and my friend bowed down really low in respect and said we have no financial means of showing our gratitude for her love, but we wanted to say that we were grateful and we will always appreciate her care. On that note we left her house and continued with our 'tour'.

A few weeks later I went to college to check on my results. I saw Mrs Adelawo, greeted her and walked away – I had only taken a few steps when she called me back and said something that I would remember for the rest of my life.

She said that she had always wanted to help students who come across as shy and this she had done for a few years. However, she continued, this is the first time that any of the many people she had had made the effort to come back and show gratitude. She said she was so honoured by our visit that she had recommended us both for special awards during the graduation ceremony.

Sometimes we seem to overlook the significant of giving heart felt gratitude. We live in a culture of 'thank you' and 'cheers'. To receive unusual favour, we need to do unusual things and one of the unusual things that we can do is give genuine gratitude and this should not necessarily be for something 'big'.

3. When size doesn't matter

So, my day started like this – I woke up, thanked God for seeing another day (even though it was a bit dark and miserable), I did a few press-ups and spent the next twenty minutes catching up with the latest news on SKY. Oops! It was time to start getting ready for work so I dragged myself to the bathroom for my usual make over, got dressed, jumped into the car and off I was on the very familiar drive to work.

I got to my new executive office which happens to be massive room that includes a separate round table where I sit to hold meetings with my team (well actually; the office belongs to the Assistant Director and I am only borrowing it until the works in the open office are done, and then I know my butt will be kicked back to the main office – but in the mean time I am loving my new status even if it's temporary). So, there I was sitting at my desk feeling cool with myself when the PA to the Director walked in and handed me two envelops. Each envelop contained a letter of confirmation of the successful completion of the probationary period of two of my team members, each signed by the director. I was so pleased about the letters that I jumped out of my seat and ran to my manager's office with delight. I was so proud and happy, not just for the two officers concerned, but for myself as well. I was particularly happy because my current position is my first managerial role and I set both officers off in their role and saw them through the successful completion of their probation.

I guess you must be wondering why on earth I was rejoicing at what could be deemed insignificant, especially as it did not relate to me directly.

You see; there are things in life that we just expect to happen.

We expect to wake up after a nights' sleep; We expect to go out on our usual business and return to base in one piece; We expect other people to be understanding towards our situations; We expect our spouses to be loving and considerate even when we sometimes do not deserve such acts; We expect that the people who supposedly look up to us will show us some form of respect; We expect gratitude from those who we show favour; We expect to be showered with praises for any good we do; We expect all staff to be confirmed into position after their six months probationary period.

Taking things for granted!

We should understand that the most exquisite diamond can easily lose its lustre with familiarity.

Unfortunately, the consequences of expecting things to just happen is that we easily get into the routine of developing an attitude that tends to make us take things for granted. The resulting effect of this is the inclination towards becoming easily disappointed by the very things that should ordinarily excite us and make us happier people. Sometimes we need to view everything that surrounds us with new eyes and live to appreciate the 'small' things.

The acquisition of your dream house, getting your dream job, finally dating the man / woman you have fancied for ages, seeing your offspring graduating from college, becoming the best selling author or seeing your business turning over millions are all things to be very happy about and proud of – but you will become more fulfilled when you appreciate the small things - you will definitely be heading towards living a happier life when 'size' seizes from being proportional to the degree of your joy. Learn to be happy just for being able to keep a job – some can't.

And I guess this explains why I was filled with joy at the thought that I have contributed (in a small way admittedly) to the success story of two co-workers of mine.

Now smile – you have just finished reading a brilliant article using your wonderful intact intellect to decode what I have been ranting on about!

4. Why don't you say it now? — Contributed by Bola Iduoze

It was my mum's birthday and I was thinking about her and all she has done and taught us her children. She has done so well and she is indeed a shinning example of the 'Bionic Woman' in Proverbs 31.

I thought about her impact in the lives of everyone she has come in contact with and as the bible says "she surpassed them all, and her children arise and call her blessed!"

I thought to myself, it is easy to know the impact of someone in your life and keep it unsaid till they are dead...at their funeral, when they can't physically hear it anymore. I didn't want to do that to my mum, she deserved to hear it and know it now! So, I picked up the phone and made the international call to tell her how I see her, as my role model! It was a great day and left me with a good, teary feeling!

So, what is the point of this story, if you have been impacted by anyone, never leave it till it's too late, tell them now!

THIRTEEN

INADEQUACIES

1. Eyes wide open

Imagine someone suddenly handing you a picture book, in this book is a collection of all the opportunities that have come your way and have passed you by because you had failed to take the appropriate action to grab them. In this book, each opportunity missed is represented diagrammatically and there is a column beneath each highlighted opportunity for you to give a reason why you missed each opportunity.

Of the many reasons that you may have put down, what reason do you think will be the most common denominator? Will the most frequent reason for missing opportunities be the fear of failing, will it be lack of knowledge, how about lack of drive, finances might have been tight, maybe the timing of the opportunity seemed inappropriate, were you discouraged by your comrades, health might be a factor, what about pure unadulterated laziness – the list could go on forever.

An underlying factor that holds many of us down and prevents us from getting a breakthrough in life is that thing in our heads that keeps telling us that we are not good enough - inadequacy.

The other day a correspondence came into our office from a Member of Parliament and my manager asked me to respond; there was no way I was going to do that. I do not think a lot of the way I write, and I was not going to embarrass myself by exposing my incompetence to some politician and thereby bring the company into disrepute. So I gave some excuse and got him to write the letter instead – big mistake!

Maybe you are one of the few that is never fazed by any situation, you might be in the minority that excel at everything they do and nothing seems like a challenge.

For the rest of the people in the world, feeling inadequate in some situations or feeling inadequate due to some personal flaws is not in itself a dire state of affair. In many circumstances it is a good thing depending on your mind-set towards your so called flaw.

About a year ago there was an inter-region football competition organised by the events team of the company I work for. I was in the team, only because there was acute shortage of men. Anyway, the match started and I found myself running around like some lunatic with no sense of direction whatsoever. While I was busy making a fool of myself, another colleague of mine was playing his heart out. He was so gracious on the field and he was declared the best player of the competition.

Did he make me feel inadequate? – No way!

I love football and I follow it religiously, I have been to many stadiums across the UK to watch the beautiful game and I play the beautiful game on Playstation at least twice every week; but that is where it ends. I never ever dreamt of playing the game, so no matter how good someone else is at it, it has nothing to do with me and I will never feel intimidated either.

On the other hand however, when I see the way some people write, I could feel a wee bit inadequate and when I hear some people talk with eloquence and elegance, I could get a bit intimidated simply because I want to get better at these things.

There are so many aspects of myself where I feel very inadequate but I've reached the decision not to fret about my inadequacies in areas that will not enhance my dream but rather enhance myself in areas where my passion lies; thereby using my shortcoming in such areas as an excuse to further develop myself.

The key issue here is that while some inadequacies should be treated as low priority with the consequences having minimal effect on your well being, some might be a bit more significant, and ignoring such shortfalls could put a dent on your future endeavours. These are the areas to which your eyes should be wide open with the will to ensuring that you get closer and closer to your dream each day.

Rather than feeling inadequate and viewing some tasks as daunting, feel challenged with the desire to take up the challenge and eventually come out at the other end a winner.

2. Jack and the Beanstalk

I went to get our older daughter from school and on our way back home she told me about her school play and how much she enjoyed it. At the end of her narration I told her that I really liked how it ended and that I love stories that end with some form of moral. I told her that when I was very young, my favourite story used to be (and still is) Jack and the beanstalk. She said she loved the story as well and we started telling each other what we liked about it.

In case you have no idea what the story is all about, or if you have forgotten, the edited version goes like this:

"A poor widow told her son to sell off the last cow they had so they could feed on the proceeds and on his way Jack met a strange man who convinced Jack to exchange the cow for five strange looking bean seeds. Jack went ahead with the swap only to get a serious telling off from his hungry and angry mum. She was angry with him for bringing five 'inadequate' bean seeds home – she would rather have the cow back! His mum sent him to bed hungry and she angrily threw the seeds into the garden.

The next day the seeds had grown into a long beanstalk which grew high up into the sky. Jack climbed the tree a couple of times and each time he came back with some very precious and expensive stuff. By the time he went up the third time, the landlord who he had been taking things from 'sourced' him out and chased poor Jack down the beanstalk. There was only so far Jack could run ahead of the landlord because he (the landlord) happened to be Shrek's great grand uncle – a giant ugly ogre. Jack got to the bottom of the beanstalk before the ogre and he yelled for his mum to hand him an axe – he cut the stem and the ogre fell to the ground and immediately started resting in peace. Jack inherited all the treasures that the ogre had greedily possessed and Jack and his mum lived happily very rich ever after".

The bean seeds, the seeds that were perceived as useless pieces of 'inadequate nothings' turned out to be the source of riches for a deprived family.

One day a timid single mum was on a train and an idea suddenly jumped into her head. She had no pen to write down her idea and she was too shy to ask the other passengers on the train for a pen. The train was delayed, and rather than thinking of constructing a complaint letter, she seized the opportunity to ponder further on her rather grand idea. She had to do this because she knew that the longer she thought about the idea, the greater the chances are that she would remember the idea for longer. She got home and wrote a few words down and the idea became bigger and better in her head with every passing day. This is a woman who while in school, was never thought of her as someone who could string letters together well enough to make a decent sentence, but as an adult she believed in her own dream, a dream that involved writing. She continued to write until her tiny thoughts became a book, and many more books followed. You might have heard about the books, they are based around a guy called Harry and the writer who remains modest despite being the richest author living is JK Rowling.

The similarity between Jack and Ms Rowling - they both had seeds that no one else believed in but the seed bearers!

Imagine Ms Rowling announcing to the fellow passengers on the train "I've got an idea; it's involves writing about some wizard, can one of you please lend me a pen!" Maybe, just maybe someone will lend her their pen, I doubt if the pen owner would want the pen back afterwards. I mean, if you lend a seemingly crazy person anything, would you want it back?

Your dream, your idea or your ambition might sound a bit strange to other people – you might feel uncomfortable expressing your heart's desire to other people because you might come across as weird; but that's perfectly ok. What will be more concerning is if you prohibit yourself from working towards your dream because you have qualified yourself as inadequate or unqualified to be the man or woman your God wants you to be.

If you do not have what it takes to be great in whatever area you desire, the idea of greatness would not have shown up in your radar in the first place.

At least 'un-disqualify' yourself – you owe your dream that much.

3. Please make me complete

I sat at my desk in the office busy doing some of the things I was being paid to do, then suddenly my phone rang; it was someone from the Human Resources department. The lady at the other end of the phone wanted to know if I have had an eye test recently – Recently? I cannot remember ever having an eye test, so the word 'recently' does not come into play here. Anyway, she said I could have one if I wanted to and it would be at the company's expense. Why not?

A few days later I was answering questions from the optician while she was busy putting different lenses on my eyes and asking me to read some letters and to look into some lights. After about half an hour of going through the ritual involved in an eye test, the optician told me that I have good eye sight (what's new), but (there is always a 'but') my sight is only good because one of the eyes compensates for the other – what? She gave me a piece of paper with an inscription typed in very tiny fonts and covered my right eye; I was able to read it perfectly. She covered the left eye and asked me to read the inscription again – this time I could not see a thing, the whole thing was blurry. She then told me to read the inscription with both eyes open and this time I could read it perfectly. Individually, one of my eyes has a defect but when I use both eyes I can see perfectly.

Do you know anyone who is perfect in everyway; or better put, do you know anyone who seems to be good at what they do. When you check such people out, they have the right sort of people around them. Anyone who seems to be anywhere near perfection commands such appearance because they associate with people who compliment their shortcomings. We are always surrounded by good people, so make no mistake about it – it is not just about surrounding yourself with good people. It is more about being wise enough to know how to tap into the resources that surround you (people resources) and allowing each resource to make a difference to your own life.

A good leader is not just good because he has good people around him. What will make him stand out is his ability to recognise the uniqueness in every individual available to him, and putting each unique talent into appropriate use to the overall effectiveness of his team.

Inadequacies

This principle is available to anyone who believes in it – for instance I have no dress sense whatsoever, hence my wife dresses me up everyday practically. This explains why I always look good despite my lack of coordination.

You are not expected to be Mr Perfecto, but having the right people around you could make up for the gap; just as you are bridging the gap for someone else – I am sure!

FOURTEEN

INFLUENCE

1. I was there

I remember some many years ago while I was in secondary school how some ex-students would write a very common phrase in strategic parts of the classroom. It would usually read something like 'Sam was here'. To those 'seniors' of mine it was a way of leaving their mark behind in the school after they had left. While I was finishing my GCSE O Level examinations I fancied doing the same thing – you know using a stone to scrabble the words 'Ayodele was here' under a desk or somewhere. I didn't do that eventually simply because I could not be bothered, and more so, I did not think I was really there. I mean was that a proper way of leaving a mark?

For the second time in the space of one week I bumped into an ex work colleague, and for some strange reason he said the same thing as the one I saw a few days earlier; 'we were talking about you the other day'. He told me that some colleagues were talking about how well I used to communicate with contemporaries which in turn made the rosters that I used to produce almost perfect. Bearing in mind that I had left the company in question about four years ago, I think I had done well.

Don't get this wrong, neither of these colleagues spoke about how well or how hard I worked. They couldn't have anyway, because I never work that hard or that well. Truly leaving a mark behind is all about how much you interact with people. I have always believed that life is all about people. I can confidently say that I can go back to any company that I have worked for and still get a good welcome at least.

I have always thought that there is no point being anywhere without leaving a stamp after your departure; be it school, church or work.

Tips on leaving a mark -

o   Live life to the fullest. Make sure you enjoy the moment in time, it will never come back and while you are happy you can only have a positive effect on those that surround you.

o   Be true and honest, begin with yourself and then extend to others.

o   Use your words wisely. Words have power and can create influence, do not spread them carelessly.

o   Become an inspiration to others – so think carefully before you speak and act.

o   Create a genuineness about you that is addictive to all those who met you.

Wouldn't it be nice to leave a mark on those you meet, a good mark that maybe would have not been left if you were not in their lives?

Now that is what leaving a mark is all about!

2. Leave them alone

A cruise ship docked in a tiny Mexican Village. While at port, an American tourist complimented a Mexican fisherman on the quality of his fish and asked him how long it took him to catch them

"Not very long" answered the Mexican.

"But then, why didn't you stay out longer and catch more?" asked the American.

The Mexican explained that the small catch was sufficient to meet his needs and the needs of his friends and the needs of his family.

The American asked "But what do you do with the rest of your time?"

"I sleep late, fish a little, play with my children, and take a siesta with my wife. In the evenings, I go into the village to see my friends, have a few drinks, play the guitar, and sing a few songs...I have a full life"

The American interrupted "Man! I have an MBA from Harvard and I can help you! You should start by fishing longer every day. You can then sell the extra fish you catch. With the extra revenue, you can buy a bigger boat. With the extra money the larger boat will bring, you can buy a second one and a third one and so on until you have an entire fleet of trawlers. Instead of selling your fish to a middle man, you can negotiate directly with the processing plants and maybe even open your own plant. You can then leave this little village and move to Mexico City, Los Angeles, or even New York City! From there you can direct your huge enterprise!"

"How long would that take?" asked the Mexican.

"Twenty, perhaps 25 years" replied the American

"and after that?"

"afterwards? That's when it really gets interesting" answered the American, laughing "When your business gets really big, you can start selling shares in it and make millions!"

"Millions! Really? After that?"

"After that you'll be able to retire, live in a tiny village near the coast, sleep late, play with your children, catch a few fish, take a siesta, and spend your evenings drinking and enjoying your friends".

"Yeah, but I do that already" said the fisherman.

We sometimes get carried away in trying to 'push' people to reach their 'destinies'. The question however is this – whose destiny are we really trying to help reach? Are we genuinely trying to help these unwilling souls or are we trying to use them to achieve our own ambitions.

I believe strongly that people need to be encouraged from time to time, myself inclusive; however some people want to be left alone because they are happy with the way they are. These people should be loved for who they happen to be because we are not all called to be Richard Branson, and a lot of people do not want to be.

3. Starting at home

I was at a Management Training Course the other week when the course tutor asked the group who they would like to influence the most. As you would expect, various answers started filling the air, ranging from some wanting to influence their subordinates, their superiors, members of their families, friends, and colleagues.

While all these rather interesting suggestions were going on, I quietly thought to myself – the one person I would love to influence the most is me! I told my small group what my thoughts were and the leader of the group relayed this to the tutor who agreed with me in totality.

So why on earth do I need to influence me?

Very easy actually – I have come to realise that I need to remind myself each time I am awake that I have a great purpose on earth and this purpose has to be achieved quickly. It is too easy for others to remind us of our shortcomings, our weaknesses and our past failings; hence the resolve. The resolve is to plant a seed of encouragement in my own dear heart each day despite all odds.

There is no denying that whatever seed you decide to sow today will germinate into the corresponding plant tomorrow. Also, charity they say starts from home, so I guess the best place to start is within us.

This should be the starting point, the month when we start to sow seeds of encouragement, seeds of happiness, seeds of assurance, seeds of positivity and seeds of progress. Start by telling yourself daily how great your future is; plant this wonderful seed in your heart by reminding yourself that no one can stop what God has started in your life and watch your seed germinate into a fruitful life.

Better still, go ahead and sow this seed into the life of others by helping them believe in their own abilities.

Job done!

4.   When push comes to shove

Everyone but Sam had signed up for the new company pension plan that called for a small employee contribution. The company was paying the rest. Unfortunately, 100% employee participation was required otherwise the plan was off.

Sam's boss and his fellow workers pleaded and cajoled Sam to participate but he refused, arguing that the plan would never pay off.

Finally the company's chief executive called Sam into his office and said, "Sam, here is a copy of the new pensions plan and here is a pen. I want you to sign the papers. I am sorry but if you do not sign the paper you are fired as of right now".

Sam signed the papers immediately.

The chief executive when on to say, "So Sam, would you mind telling me why you couldn't have signed the papers earlier?"

"Well sir", said Sam, "nobody explained it to me quite so clearly before".

We deal with various people in various aspects of our lives, this leads to the fact that we deal with various personalities and attitudes. This will also lead to the fact that in the quest for you and me to have a good relationships with people we need to treat everyone differently depending on the nature of the person that we are dealing with.

Whether you're looking to improve a love relationship, familial relationships, friendships, or work relationships, understanding your own personality type and the personality type of the other person involved in the relationship will bring a new dynamic to the situation, which will allow better understanding and communication. Although the different types of relationships have very different characteristics and specific needs, there are two basic areas which seem to be critical in all relationships:

1. Expectations and
2. Communication.

What do we expect from ourselves and the other person involved in the relationship? How do we communicate these expectations, and our feelings and opinions to the other person in the relationship? How does our personality type affect our expectations and methods of communication? Does our personality type affect who we are romantically attracted to? How does it affect who our friends are, and who we work with best?

When it comes to work colleagues, or friends, we are not especially interested in dealing with people who are very unlike ourselves. We are most comfortable with those who have similar interests and perspectives, and we do not show a lot of motivation or patience for dealing with our opposites.

The better we become in dealing successfully with those who are not very much like we 'want them to be', the greater the chances that we will be able to widen our circle of influence.

FIFTEEN

INITIATIVE

1. It's only a console

The problem of growing up!

We get older, and we assume this guarantees wisdom, intelligence and everything that is associated with growing older. Maybe growing up makes us wiser, but on the other hand it makes us become too aware, and our awareness could sometimes lead us to becoming too conscious of who and what is around us which in turn restricts our sense of creativity and initiative.

Watch children play, the way they create a whole heap of 'rubbish' from nothing is phenomenal. They will ask for anything from paper to boxes and create something that only they can explain. It doesn't stop there – they come up with ideas that as adults we easily dismiss rather than applaud the acumen they display.

Unfortunately, as soon as they start to grow up they become 'normal'.

It's a shame really.

I was watching TV with the missus one evening when our eight year old daughter came to us and said that almost everyone in her class owned a console called Nintendo DX and she wanted one as well. She looked towards her mum who completely ignored her. She turned to me and I told her that I simply could not afford what she wanted. She showed her displeasure by frowning and she went to her bedroom in annoyance. We thought we had got rid of her; but lo and behold there she was a few minutes later right in front of us – however, this time her frown was replaced with a massive smile.

95

"Mummy, you know you always stay up late to do the dishes. As from tonight I will help you with the dishes and you will pay me £1". We were still puzzled, and she was still beaming when she said "Also mummy, I will get up early every morning to help you look for your shoes and this service will cost you another £1". She now looked my way, while I feared the worst she said "Daddy, I will be your helper every Saturday when you wash the cars and my service will cost you £1 each time".

We agreed to her proposal, at least to get rid of her. Before she went to bed she did some work in the kitchen and came back to ask for her 'payment'. This trend continued for months and she would even ask for payment for some ridiculous things such as helping put out the rubbish.

One Saturday evening she walked up to me and said that she needs to buy her console – I asked to see her 'collection' and yours truly, she was only a few pounds short of the cost of the Nintendo DX. Her aunty made up the difference, and we were so proud of her that I rushed out and got her what she wanted.

An adult would get refused a request, accept the negative response and move on. We get rejected for a job, we look for another one, and another one and the trend will go on forever. Our creativity diminishes as we get older.

One of the best things we could do to help us achieve our dreams is reverse our minds and sometimes remind ourselves of what we were like as children.

It might just be a console, but the same principle applies to the law of creativity and initiative.

2. The extra mile

Where do you see yourself in a few years, and even more importantly, what physical and spiritual processes have you put in place to get there?

One of the many things that I see myself becoming is a successful writer and a well known speaker. I see copies of my books displayed in major bookshops across the country. I wish that one day I will be invited to a well known bookshop to sign copies of one of my books and there will be a long queue of people waiting for my autograph. I look forward to the time that one of my books will be listed as a bestseller.

Looking forward to dreams and wishing they come true – that is the easy bit. The question here is what have I been doing to making such dreams come to past?

I will usually visualise these things happening in my life and I will even go a step further and act as if they have already manifested. I will sometimes walk into bookshops and use my imagination to see books written by Ayodele Olusanya on display. I also see my book getting a very good review in newspapers. Then the next stage of my dreams involve seeing myself addressing a massive crowd and getting standing ovations at various stages during my speech.

I guess that I must state that I have already written a book and I am in the process of completing my second book – so it is not just about dreaming.

I did something else last Thursday in preparedness of my dream for the future coming true. I went to Waterstones in Bluewater and bought a book. I then joined a long queue of people waiting for their books to be autographed. While I was standing in the queue I was saying prayers. My prayers when something like this.

"Heavenly father, I want to thank you for giving me a dream to pursue, thank you for giving me the grace to take my dreams to another level. As I stand in this queue waiting for an autograph, I pray that one day not too far away, I will be at the other end of the queue waiting for people to come to me for my signature on the copies of my book that they have bought. I pray to you heavenly Father to make me a platform to display the talents that you have blessed me with and I will continue to give you all the glory – Amen".

By the time I said this prayer over and over again it was my turn to get to meet the presenter of Sunrise on SKY news and National Lottery Jet set for BBC1 and involve him in a few minutes conversation before he signed a copy of his book for me in which he wrote "to Ayodele, great to meet you, cheers".

As I walked away from the bookshop I continued to pray that my time comes soon. This was a physical and spiritual activity that I embarked on so that I can get to my Canaan.

It was an 'Extra Mile' that I decided to take to get there, what extra mile will you be taking to aid your journey to progression?

SIXTEEN

JOY

---

1. I have an unusual nose

Let us take a trip down memory lane.

When you were in primary school, did you ever think that you would be a bit more fulfilled once you got into secondary school? Was that the case?

When you passed out of secondary school, were you looking forward to life in the world of higher education, expecting it to bring you all the contentment and fun that goes with it; and did it? Maybe you are now employed – are you truly in high spirits at work? How about at home or with your friends; and how do you feel about life generally? Do you think you would be a bit happier if things could change a wee bit? Maybe you would actually; the only bother is the how long the euphoria will last for after the necessary changes to your life have been implemented.

I remember some very many years ago, I walked into my room at the Polytechnic and a member of the social club I belonged to handed me a report that I had asked him to put together. I looked at what he had produced for a few seconds and with a smile I looked at him and said "This is beautiful". Everyone in the room burst into laughter, and I stood there thinking, what was funny? "We have all said that once you come in and see the document you would say that it was beautiful, and you did", one of them told me. I guess they have found out that it does not take a whole lot to please me – I must be cheap.

Many of us are happy; there is no doubt about that. The only concern is what exactly makes us happy, how long we are happy for and how much effort we have to put into being happy. If for instance you find yourself beaming from ear to ear because you have finally bought your dream car, how long will you drive the car for before it ceases to be a reason for you to smile? This is where the power of 'joy' comes in.

What exactly is the difference between joy and happiness?

Happiness is derived from doing, observing or achieving something that you like, while joy is the connection with the source of life within you. While happiness is usually momentary, joy is continuous.

The main difference between happiness and joy is that while happiness is very much dependent on something or someone outside of yourself; joy is self facilitating and it comes from within. Ok, let us forget all the rambling above and put it this way – happiness requires endeavour, whereas joy is effortless. Like every other thing, continual practice will make things that seem difficult become much more part of our nature. But what exactly do we need to practice on in order to make us joyful and fulfilled for almost ever?

I am not entirely satisfied with my job, but while it's what I have at the minute, I have decided to look beyond the actual job and appreciate the little things that come with the job; so when my workload seems daunting, rather than getting miserable I get out of my seat, take a walk to other departments to have 'a little laugh'. For some strange reason the environment (and not necessarily the people) around me seems to respond positively when I create the atmosphere I wish to have around me. This is a formula I have adopted throughout most of my adult life and it always pays off.

The consequence of appreciating the small things around me is rather straight forward; my happiness is independent of my environment because I create the environment I desire; my financial situation has nothing to do with my outlook, I will always have a smile to spend; my happiness is not dependent on people's opinion about me because I was not designed to meet their expectations; and I have consciously decided to appreciate little things like the rather unusual shape of my nose. You might think my nose looks funny, but I have had it for over forty years and it gives me joy because it stands out (literally).

Find 'little' things to appreciate, things like the design of your office building, or the various functions on your mobile phone, or the beauty of how people with diverse backgrounds live together without punching each others lights out.

Trust me, appreciating the 'small' things that surround you will give you permanent happiness; otherwise called Joy.

2. Just laugh

The best medicine they say is laughter; how true.

I have always wondered why people do not laugh enough and I still cannot figure out why. My wife always says that I can laugh for England, and how true she is. I try to walk around with a smile and this is not necessarily because I always have a reason to be in high spirits, it's because I have decided within myself to make a conscious effort to be happy.

Be happy!

We owe ourselves that much. There are too many negative factors that surround us and they keep giving us 'good' reasons to be unhappy. They come in different forms and they are transmitted by various people. I appreciate how challenging it is to maintain a happy as Larry attitude at all times, but when you dig deep you will find some things to be happy about. Bring these tiny aspects of your life to the surface of your heart and be grateful that you are still standing, then smile or even laugh.

I once had a serious attack of malaria. It was so bad that I had to do one of the things that I really do not like doing; I had to go to the doctors. This was about twenty years ago while I was still living with my mum in the lovely city of Lagos. My condition was so bad that I could hardly walk for more than five minutes without having to take a break. My mum dropped me off at the doctors and she headed off to work. This meant that had to take a bus back home after my treatment. I left the clinic at about 11am when the weather was at its hottest and this only made my condition worse.

I boarded a bus and started my long journey home.

It was a massive bus, and at the back of each seat was a metal handle which ran across the entire length of the seats. I was sitting alongside two gentlemen one was busy reading a newspaper and the other was busy sleeping.

I was sitting there feeling weak, tired, and very ill and I could hardly speak. I had an extremely high temperature and I was not in a smiling or laughing mood. My condition meant that it would take a miracle to make me laugh. The ride in the bus was a rocky one to say the least. The driver was not sure if he had human beings as his passengers or a pack of animals by the way he drove. He kept applying the brakes whenever he felt like. At one point the driver applied the brakes and the guy sleeping hit his forehead against the metal piece in front of him with some intense force. Bang!

A few minutes later and Bang! he hit his head against the metal piece again and miraculously he continued in his sleep. Minutes later literally and Bang! At this stage the man sitting next to the man with the head said in a very loud voice "old boy, your head strong o" (my friend, you have a strong head!)

For a moment my sickness left me. I burst into uncontrollable laughter. We were on the bus for another twenty minutes and I could not stop smiling. I forgot my pain for as long as I was laughing or smiling. I got home and every time I remembered the 'bus incident' I would laugh my sorrows away. 20% of the factors that contributed to my recovery were to do with the medication the doctor gave me; the other 80% was from the laugher in my heart.

I know it may be difficult, it maybe hard, it may even seem impossible, but I need you try something new this week. Leave your troubles to a side for most (possibly for the whole) of the week and spend time doing things that make you happy, things that make you smile and things that make you laugh. At the end of the week; spot the difference in your life.

3. Look around – contributed by Bola Iduoze

Red Skelton, wrote…

"I live by this credo: Have a little laugh at life and look around you for happiness instead of sadness. Laughter has always brought me out of unhappy situations. Even in your darkest moment, you can usually find something to laugh about if you try hard enough."

I know that if you look hard enough, you will see something to laugh at in an unhappy situation, and you will see something that creates joy in your heart in a very sad situation. This therefore means you feel what you see.

So, go ahead and give it a try, the next time you are faced with an unhappy situation, look for something that will make you laugh.

SEVENTEEN

LEADERSHIP

1. Follow me – contributed by Ijapari Haman

Our heart is the well spring of life, when we contain things like insecurities, hatred, being inhuman, not being considerate to other people, choosing who to love…it is such little things that reveal what is hidden in our hearts. God normally looks for how we react to small things; it speaks volumes on what is stored in our hearts. Saul was a man full of insecurities, he couldn't allow other people that God was raising under him to grow- 1 Samuel 18, he chased after David with the intention to take his life. As a leader, you are required to be secure in your position so that you are able to multiply yourself, rather than put down the people you are meant to be leading.

The leadership of Jesus Christ depicts how genuine love and a growing leadership can change the lives of your team.

Leadership is influence, nothing more, nothing else. Being a leader means you have at least one follower. The title leadership does not mean a thing if your followers are still in the same position you meet them in. The real issue is what you do with your leadership. That's what really counts.

'Leadership is measured by the markers on the journey. It's not where you take them, but how you got them there and what shape they were in when they arrived that demonstrated good leadership'

Mark 1:16- "Follow me."

With those two simple words, Jesus transformed the lives of His disciples and ultimately changed the world. Leaders, by definition, have followers. As one wise commentator put it, if no one is following you, you're not leading; you're just taking a walk!

2. Tell me why

Leading becomes easier when the followers know that the one leading has some form of honour imbedded inside them.

Integrity is so important to a leader that it needs to be a conscious and daily decision for you, if you intend to lead. Integrity is the foundation that God builds a successful life upon. Integrity and prosperity go hand in hand in the mind of God. The catch is that you have to be faithful and full of integrity even in the things that seem insignificant. God will bless you when you maintain honesty, integrity, and faithfulness to Him in all things you do, whether great or small.

3. The courageous you – contributed by Olamide Sanni

I am reminded of the story of a woman whose courage has become a historical landmark and a point of reference. Queen Esther in her time was a woman who transformed the plights of a country by simply unleashing her courage during the restless period that her people lived in. The entire nation of Israel had been written off by their enemies, and though she was hardly seen as a threat, she had audaciously requested that her people's lives be preserved, thereby using her influence very courageously to absolve them [Esther 7:3-4].

Esther's bold impulse to expose the misleading conspiracy behind the entire decision was the fine line between doing what is referred to in the Bible as standing in the gap, and refusing to allow evil overthrow the innocent lives of her people. Her courage preserved the whole of Israel.

The necessities for a successful life, full of impact and significance hinge mainly on the extraordinary power of courage, as this in itself gives room to strong attributes such as assertiveness, truthfulness and the audacity to pursue dreams and visions. Courage is a simple, yet very potent means of making a big difference. Many times, we believe that it represents the total absence of fear or the inexistence of anxiety. But in my experience, courage is only known and has always been best reflected in tough situations despite the possibility of dire mishaps.

4. Who cares

People do not care about what you know, they what to know how much you care.

Empathy is simply feeling what others feel, and then letting them know that you care about them by the loving way you treat them. It sounds easy enough, but it's usually harder to practice compassion than it is to talk about it. But by following the leadership style of Christ, you are more than capable of being a compassionate person each day. All that you have to do is to be sensitive to the leading of the Spirit, and follow directions when He prompts you to act towards someone in need. You have that "small voice" inside of you that tells you what you should do. Just listen to it! When you understand what people are going through, then you can understand their needs.

These are the attributes that stand you out as the true leader.

EIGHTEEN

MOTIVATION

1. Pay your dream a visit

There are two good reasons why a grown man should cry; when something rather tragic happens, and when he finally achieves his hearts desire after a being faced with a succession of obstacles and failures.

I know a guy all too well.

He was born in the late 60's in the UK and his parents and two junior sisters left for Africa in the mid 70's. He had his primary, secondary and higher education in Africa, and got his first job as a laboratory technician, and life was – oh well, not very good. My dear friend was being paid close to peanuts and the peanuts were used to travel to and from work which meant that at the end of every month he was left penniless. The job itself had no prospects and no matter what he tried to change his job, he kept being told that he did not have enough experience, or he was not good enough. He dare not imagine dating anyone simply because he never had enough money to take them out with – anyway he had to look good first, and even that was an issue. To buy a shirt or two at the end of any month, he would have had to skip breakfast and lunch for at least three weeks consecutively and rely on mamas cooking in the evening.

After a few years of toiling in vain, the young man decided to go into the business of manufacturing and selling. He went out to borrow money to fund his 'business' of making and selling soap. In the process of making the soap he got some severe burns from the caustic soda, the burns that almost left him 'marked' for life. The worse bit was that no one was willing to buy the soap, leaving him in even more debt. At this time, he was suffering from a terrible heart condition that could have easily cost him his life. Simply put, things were not very good.

So he had to take another line of action – go 'back' to the UK and hope to start all over again. He applied for his passport at the British consulate. This was going to be easy, he thought to himself – it took only three to four weeks for his sisters to obtain theirs. After about two months of applying, he was invited for an initial interview – oh yeah! As you might have rightly thought his application was refused. He had to apply again, and this time there was another big bang when the same passport was given the 'refused' stamp. My friend was left heart broken; nothing seemed to go well in his life. One day, a friend of his was coming from the UK so he went to the international airport in Lagos to welcome him. As he was waiting at the airport watching various sorts of people coming and going, he started to ponder on whether his time would ever come. In his heart he was happy for those who were 'lucky' enough to be able to get what it took to fly out of the country. He genuinely prayed for them with all his heart and he would end by saying that one day the British Commission people will show mercy and he would be able to come to the airport and travel to the UK. Then an idea came to his head; "maybe I should visit the airport frequently and use it as a prayer point for my dreams" So he did. At least once a month, he would finish from work and head to the airport. He would stand by the entrance and start to day dream; he will be pondering on when he would be able to come to the airport to catch a real flight. He did this over and over and over again – each time feeling happy for those travelling and praying fervently for himself. One day, he went on his usual trip to the airport only to discover that there was no means of getting home – this would not dampen his spirit. After the usual hanging around the departure lounge, he started a very long trek home, walking for hours before a bus emerged from only God knows where. While walking he was trying to remember as many happy faces at the airport as possible, rejoicing with each one of them and using them as a prayer point for himself.

Then one day, he went to the airport, walked through the departure lounge, checked himself in (what luggage?) and did something unimaginable – he boarded a plane, a plane destined for London. When he sat in his allocated seat, he started to ponder on his insane trips to the airport and then the tears manifested.

It was insane, but sometimes playing insanity is sanity by itself. Maybe you want to pay your dream a visit from time to time, it might just be tonic you need.

2. What is your reference point?

In 1897 Johnson Oatman, Jr. in his popular song asked us to count our blessings and name them one by one – that's fair enough I guess. There are times however when the 'not very pleasant' times in your life should play a very important role in motivating you.

I know a man who is certain that his children will do great exploits and whenever someone dares to ask him where he gets his confidence from, he tells them the same old story. One day he came back home from work to be told that a massive fire had engulfed his children's bedroom and this all happened while his three children were deep in sleep. The man (who happens to be my dad) broke down in tears when it dawned on him that he almost lost his children (including yours truly), at very early stages of their lives. Even though this happened about thirty years ago, whenever I go through a difficult time, his usual phrase will be "the God that saved you from the flames and got you out without any burns will see you through this situation". The man always refers back to a very difficult period in his life and uses it as a prayer reference and motivational tool.

During one of our recent mid week prayer meetings, a lady told the rest of the group of how she was continually tormented by her partner over her 'inability' to have children. Her partner already had children from a previous relationship, so he knew the problem was not from him. Even her partner's close relatives would join in on the act of inflicting the lady with pain and anguish at the time she could have done with some support. There were times when she would sob night and day and have no one to share her sorrows with. Everything else in her life was put on hold because her whole existence was then geared towards having a baby and nothing else mattered. Months went by, prayers were said and scriptures were read, years when by and more prayers were said and more scriptures were read. One day she discovered that someone was growing inside her – her dream came true. She now has two children and things looked good until another challenge came her way and she was at the brink of losing her home. Guess what she did! She remembered the time she was praying fervently for a child and she used the positive result she got at the end of a rather difficult time as a reference point and she believed strongly that the same God who blessed her womb would come through for her and save her home – and as you might have guessed the house is still very much hers.

There will be times when we will not have to face difficult times, but by the time those moments come we would be lifeless. As long there is still life in you, as long as you have a desire there will always be times when things would seem rather impossible. However; contrary to what the norm might be, those rather harsh memories are to be cherished.

The best motivator you will ever know is you!

The one person who has truly experienced the struggles you have faced in the past is you, you know where you have been beaten and bruised and only you can truly tell the effect of such anguish and temporary set backs in your life. Do just think of such times and make a sign of relieve and think that it only just happened for the sake of it.

Dig real deep and you will always find a moment in your life that will motivate and encourage you to higher heights. If you are reading this article, you must be of an age where you must have overcome many obstacles in the past that many other people would have not been able to surmount. You must have gone through some situations that you would have found difficult to bear, but the main thing is that you came through. Now that you have successfully emerged from a thorny situation, when another one comes – you owe it to yourself to remind yourself that you are a conqueror and even though the past problem might be petite compared to the present you and your God are able to overcome – and you will.

You know what; our previous successes could sometimes be the barrier to future successes. You cannot afford the luxury of dwelling on the past goodies in your life for too long. We need to sometimes think back to how we dealt with a difficult period and use such instances as a pivot for the better tomorrow.

If you did it before, you are stronger and more equipped to do it again – so wake up and live!

3. Write a book

I know that you have dreams and aspirations – and then obstacles rear their ugly heads!

There is no denying the fact that you have faced various brick walls along the way in trying to achieve some of the goals that you have set for yourself; that is if your dreams are big enough. The obstacles could come in various forms and shapes, from rejection to disapproval to denial to negative responses or comments; and worst of all – having no self belief. We are constantly surrounded with 'good' enough reasons to give up the fight. There are loads of factors which seem to be powerful enough in acting as stumbling blocks that serve as hindrances which aim to put a stop to whatever we set out to do.

So you had every hope of moving to the next level at work, you knew you were qualified and experienced enough to move up, even your colleagues knew you had what it takes to be at the next level and so did your managers. You applied for the post, had what you considered a good interview and yet you were rejected – someone with a bit more experience beat you to the position. You put in for what you considered your dream house. The house had everything you had always desired and there was no reason why you could not get the house. Everything was going smoothly until you received a call from your broker informing you that your mortgage application had been refused due to some credit issues. You know you have a good voice and very good stage presence; however, you simply cannot get a recording deal no matter what method you had applied. You might have started a small business, but only your Uncle James and Aunty Jenny patronised you and eventually you had to close shop – for good. Maybe you have been trying to change your career, and it you are beginning to wonder if all the stress is worth your while.

Various failings and rejections have a way of remaining in our subconscious without us knowing. They can easily become 'hold back factors' when you want to take an advancing step in life. You subconsciously start to remember all the failings of the past and then ask yourself if it is worth putting yourself through the pain again. In your mind you have already written a book – a catalogue of failings has been documented and the mind opens the book anytime you need to make a progressive move.

What is the best way to keep this 'catalogue of failings' from becoming a hindering factor – get physical!

For some strange reason, we have decided to remember some negative incidents in our lives and let go of some of the maybe smaller, but highly effective positives that have taken place in the past. So, I want to encourage us to start writing a new book. Whenever someone passes the most insignificant, but positive comment, write it down. If someone says to you in passing 'I think you have a good smile'- write it in the 'good news book'. When you get an email or even the old fashioned letter from someone telling you that you did something well; put it in the 'good news book'. When your child tells you that you are the best parent in the world – it should go in the 'good news book'. When someone tells you that you have good manners – write it in the 'good news book'. Collect all these positive comments and keep them safe. When next you are faced with an uphill task, when next you have to revisit a situation where you had previously failed, when the situation seems to be tough and rough, when you are feeling down, low in spirit and feeling like the world is against you – bring out the 'good news book', read it and remind yourself that you are a winner – then watch how your spirit gets lifted in preparedness for the task ahead.

Oh yeah, least I forget – please remember to say positive things to others too so that they could put them in their own 'good news book' as well.

NINETEEN

OPPORTUNITY

1. Loose yourself

If I were to ask you this week to look back over your life and find an event or an opportunity that you regret missing out on, I am sure every one of us can find at least one missed opportunity.

The Bible gives many examples of missed opportunities, and below are a few:

o   In the Old Testament the Israelites missed out on the opportunity of entering the Promised Land early because they discovered 'giants' when they sent spies in to search out the land.

o   A rich young ruler in the New Testament missed out on the gift of eternal life because he was too attached to his wealth. And as a result, the Bible tells us that he went away sad.

o   In the words of Jesus, in the parable of the ten virgins, five were foolish and did not bring enough oil and when the bridge groom finally arrived they missed out on the Great Wedding Feast.

o   I wonder in the four Gospels how many people missed out on the opportunity for healing because they didn't go to where Jesus was for whatever reason.

And the list goes on.

The mysterious aspect of taking opportunities is that we are never quite sure what the outcome of the 'risk' will be.

Let us spend a few minutes looking at some of the ways we could stay in tune by seizing the opportunities that come our way;

o   You will most likely not miss your opportunity if you will follow God even if you don't know exactly where He is leading you. God didn't tell Noah that it was going to rain 40 days and 40 nights until after the ark was completed.

o   You will most likely not miss your opportunity if you stay obedient to God. Lot's wife through her disobedience missed her opportunity to leave Sodom and Gomorrah before God sent down fire and brimstone.

o   You will most likely not miss your opportunity if you are not looking for your opportunity. Do you know why we don't win more souls for the kingdom of God? It is because we are not looking for the opportunity to win a soul for to God.

o   You will most likely not miss your opportunity if you can believe that it doesn't have to be big to be good. That small tug at your heart during the invitation may be your big opportunity. And if you sense that small tug at your heart then you need to take that step to the altar.

o   You will most likely not miss your opportunity if you have learned to be faithful in the opportunities that have come your way in the past. Doesn't the Scripture tell us if we are faithful in small things, God will place us in charge of large things?

Opportunities – loose yourself free from the fear of taking risk and grab the opportunities that come you way.

2.   What's in your wallet?

Where is the one place where we would find the greatest amount of untapped human talents and skills? The graveyard!

We get born, get some form of education; get a job, get hitched, have a number of children, maybe grandchildren and then its pension time and before you could say Penmaenmawr it is appointment time with the creator. However, many of us live out the active parts of our lives being unfulfilled, simply because our in born talents are crying within us for exposure, but we are too occupied to listen to the inner voice. Everyone is born with a special ability, a peculiar talent that might not necessarily make you rich or famous, but will definitely bring you an enormous sense of purpose and fulfilment. It is one thing to know that a particular talent is embedded within you; it is a more demanding task to ensure that your special ability is exposed for others to see and appreciate. Blow your own trumpet! If you don't who do you think has the time or resolve to blow it for you?

I know a guy who is gifted with a very deep voice and his eloquence is also very exceptional. He knew he had been gifted with something special because people would always tell him of his gifting, just like you are told of yours by many. He was living an unfulfilled live, maybe just like you are. His life seemed ok; he had a job driving the London underground trains around east and central London. He earned a reasonable wage, but there was always something within him yawning to come out, his talent. So, one evening he decided to take out his frustration on his passengers. He was on the late shift and his train was approaching its terminal station when he decided to play a prank. He turned off the lights in the train carriages and made an announcement in a very deep voice. He said, "Ladies and gentlemen, we are approaching Charing Cross; let us hope that this train remembers to stop. This is your driver speaking, or is it; Ha! Ha!! Ha!!!"

Obviously, many of the commuters were a bit frightened by his prank and by the next morning loads of complaint letters were on his managers' desk. He was obviously reprimanded for his action; but among the many complains was a request from one of the passengers to meet with the driver. When the driver and the curious passenger finally met some weeks later, a deal was stuck and this passenger who turned out to be the marketing director of and advertising firm introduced the 'driver' to a new world. Whenever you hear a deep voice doing the adverts on TV, it is probably the voice of the 'former train driver'. His life was changed for good, for ever.

So why the transformation; the guy decided to expose his God given gift for the world to see. Many of us are paid the same compliments by different people at different times, but what do we do – we say the same boring; 'Thank you' and walk away like nothing has happened. Why don't we spend this a moment to evaluate the things that have been said to us in the past, find out what we are truly exceptionally good at and map out strategies to expose them to the world?

I have been told many times by various people that I have a unique and artistic style of public speaking. After a few comments about my 'talent' I decided to look for means of exposing myself (nothing obscene) at every opportunity; I actually hunt around for opportunities. I have told my managers numerous times to please allow me do presentations at work. I have done a few and I will be doing my biggest presentation in a few weeks where I will be addressing my colleagues, my managers and directors - I simply cannot wait! I had also been told that I have the ability to tell motivating stories; and that was how the idea of my books and my website were conceived.

So what has been continuously said to you that you are good at, what compliments are paid to you the most, what do you do that gives you so much joy and satisfaction, better still; what's in your wallet?

Share it with the world.

3. Whoever you are – Thank you!

I want to express my gratitude to someone; I have no recollection of what the name of the gentleman is but I want to say thank you to him and I pray that God will continue to bless him in all his endeavours.

He is a very good man!

It was about thirty years ago. I was very young and did what all guys of my age range would do, play about, run around and try to fit in. One day, I was meant to be getting ready for school, but instead I was playing a game of football with the boys. I intended to kick the ball, but I stuck my right foot against a massive stone instead. Ouch! I was not wearing any footwear so maybe now you could understand the intensity of the pain I felt.

A boy's got to do what a boy's got to do.

I continued to play until it was time to head for school. I felt some pain but I did not think a lot of it. I continued my day as much as a boy with one fully functional foot could, until it was time to go home. But when it was time to go home there was a problem – I could not walk; I could not raise my right foot one bit. The leg was swollen and the pain was unbearable.

Oh dear! How do I get home?

I had to walk about a mile to get to the bus stop and I could only hop on one foot at best. My classmates and other students saw me in pure agony, but they only wished me well and went on their way. The teachers were no better. I resigned to spending about three hours trying to get home when a classmate, a guy that I hardly talked to walked towards me and offered to help. He soon lifted me up and put me on his back and walked all the way to the bus stop. He would stop a few times to get some rest and catch his breath, and then up again, I would go on his back. This continued for over an hour and when we got to the bus stop he offered to get on the bus with me and give me another 'lift' from the bus stop to our house. An elderly gentleman offered to help me get home which meant that my classmate could go home.

What a guy!

What opportunities do we wish for? Opportunities to make money, opportunities to be famous, opportunities for promotion; however this guy grabbed the opportunity to help a classmate in distress.

He took a good opportunity; it is turn for me to take one, even though, I'm taking the opportunity about thirty years later; I am taking the opportunity to pray for the boy, who by now would have turned man.

"Heavenly Father, I want to ask you to look at the kind man described above with mercy. Bless him in his goings and his comings. Grant him his heart desires and show him unwarranted mercies. May his path through life be made easy, and may he find mercy in the eyes of man. Bless his family and his friends and please heavenly father, never leave him alone – Amen".

I really don't know who he is, but I want to take this opportunity to say 'Thank You'!

TWENTY

PERSEVERANCE

1. Nothing Wasted

If you have ever had the drive to do anything exceptional in life, you can probably think of many things you have invested time, energy and money in. Many things which seemed to have profited you nothing.

It comes with the territory unfortunately; however, God's Word promises that nothing you do for His name is ever wasted! God knows and uses everything you do for His name, no matter how small the act itself may seem, and the good news is that your work for God is never in vain. Sometimes, you may not get to see the good that your efforts are producing. Our human tendency is to want to see the finished product; otherwise, we don't feel that anything has really been accomplished. But take heart, because God doesn't overlook anything you do for Him.

So, when you embark on your next project, put God first asking for His hand in what you are aiming to achieve and better still, dedicate the outcome to God – success guaranteed!

2. Soon Come

Sometimes it seems you are alone, doesn't it?

I am guessing that there seems to be a problem waiting for you no matter where you turn? Do you sometimes wonder if your dreams are ever going to come to pass? Maybe you've asked why God would allow you to struggle in your job, your relationships, your health, or some other area of life. Trust me, you are not alone.

As it says in the second book of Corinthians, 4:17 "our present troubles are quite small and won't last very long. Yet they produce for us an immeasurably great glory that will last forever"!

God allows you to go through challenges because He knows it's the struggle of life that builds strength in you. If God simply delivered you from every struggle every time, then you may not continue to grow and learn to trust Him. When you persevere through difficult times, you'll begin to realise a greater level of joy, peace, victory, and abundance than you ever dreamed possible. Remember, God loves you too much to leave you where you are. He's preparing you for something, and as awful as it may sound, perseverance is a requirement.

TWENTY ONE

PERSISTENCE

1. I did it

A young boy was sent to bed by his father.

(Five minutes later)

"Da-aaad….."
"What?" replied the dad.
"I'm thirsty. Can you please bring me a drink of water?"
"No. You had your chance. Lights out."

(Five minutes later)

"Da-aaaaaaaaaad….."
"What?"
"I'm thirsty. Can I have a drink of water?"
"I told you no! If you ask me again, I will have to spank you!"

(Five minutes later)

"Daaaaaaa-aaaaaaaaaaaaAAAAAAAAAAAAAAD………………"
"WHAT?!"
"When you come in to spank me, can you bring me a drink of water?"

Just like my colleagues at work, I have struggled with my in-tray, found it difficult to cope with the amount of emails in my in-box and it has been a struggle to cope with my work load. I was offered a new job a few weeks ago within the same company but it meant that I had to move to a different office. I was not going to leave without clearing out my in-tray, my emails and getting on top of my workload. My aim did not stop me from doing my usual stuff or taking more work on, the only difference here was that I was determined to go the extra yard.

By the end of work on my last day I had one document in my in-tray, I had four emails in my in-box from the hundreds that I usually had and I was on top of other aspects of my job as humanly possible. So how was I able to achieve this for the first time in two years?

You will be surprised at how much you will be able to achieve if you put your mind to it and stay focused. You could complain from now until kingdom comes or just get on with it with the full intention of getting your desired result, the choice is always entirely yours and no one can influence your decision.

The last four weeks were difficult, I must confess. I took no lunch occasionally and sometimes I had to stay a bit late to get more stuff done – but at least I got there at last.

Determination – sometimes is defined as the process of making a decision; however what is the point of deciding if you are not going to be resolute enough to see that decision through. Even though, sometimes you might be at the risk of getting a spanking just to get a drink of water.

2. The fear of falling again

My daughter insisted that I had to be at her schools sports day one Friday, but I really did not want to attend. Coincidentally, I had Friday off from work so I had no genuine excuse but I had my reasons why I did not want to be at her sports day. I knew there was going to be a parent's race, and that was my fear, even though I could not bring myself to telling my daughter (or even my wife) this.

Some 15 years ago I was doing my 'Youth Service' in Nigeria. (This is a scheme where you have to work for the government for 12 months after your higher education). I was working as a secondary school teacher, preparing the final year students for their GCSC examinations in Chemistry. During the sports day, I took part in the teachers' race.

We all lined up waiting for the call to start and there I was feeling cool with myself. I was lined in the middle lane, I had a glimpse of those on my right and another glimpse of those on my left – I will easily take these ones' out, I thought to myself.

GO! Shouted the guy with the rather loud voice, and we all took off. I was doing rather well, over the first 50 metres of the 200 meter distance I think I was in the second place. By the time we reached the 100 meter mark I was 3rd, and then the crucial point of the race set in. We were about 25 meters to the finishing line and I was 'sitting' comfortably in the 2nd position when disaster struck. For some strange reason, I lost my footing and before you could say 'Jack Robinson' I was laying flat on the floor after taking a rather very embarrassing tumble.

I remained on the ground while the rest of the 'athletes' finished the race. I was so embarrassed – I really was. Being laughed at by the unsympathetic students did not help either. I eventually got up, cleaned the 'sand' from my body, including the rather large quantity my mouth had taken up and vowed to never take part in another race – I was getting a bit too old for it anyway.

So I guess now you understand why I was a bit apprehensive when my little girl wanted me to take part in the father's race at her schools sports day.

When I did it so many years ago and plummeted, I was alone. The only one that carried the shame was me, myself and I. The only people present on that faithfully day were my students and fellow teachers.

This time it was a bit more complicated. I was going to run the risk of running the risk of 'falling' in the presence of my daughter, my daughter's friends, loads of other parents and teachers. My daughter would not hear the last of it if her precious day took a tumble.

The moment came; they called on 'willing' fathers' to line up for the last and grandest event of the day – fathers' race. I was the first one out, and then about 15 other very fit men took their stand. I was thinking to myself, God please 'I shall fall not'. Then GO! She shouted. I got to the finishing line and I was even given a sticker with the inscription 3rd Position written on it.

My daughter was (and still is) so proud.

The fear of 'trying again' after initial failures and embarrassments; we all go though this rather negative phenomenon from time to time. We could find ourselves in situations where we resist making progress in certain areas of our lives because of former rejections, disappointments and failure. The question here is, is it worth trying again – because even if there is the slightest likelihood that you could come out of the other end triumphant then I think you should hold your head high up and try again – who knows, you might even make yourself and someone else proud by winning a prize.

3. The well has to be dug – Contributed by Ayoola Olusanya

Genesis 26:19-22: "Isaac's servants dug in the valley and discovered a well of fresh water there. But the herdsmen of Gerar quarrelled with Isaac's herdsmen and said, "The water is ours!" So he named the well Esek, because they disputed with him. Then they dug another well, but they quarrelled over that one also; so he named it Sitnah. He moved on from there and dug another well, and no one quarrelled over it. He named it Rehoboth, saying, "Now the LORD has given us room and we will flourish in the land."

We have the tendency to give up our goals, aspirations and visions because of oppositions. At times the empty shout of the "Goliath" scares the hell out of us and we run away from the battlefield. We abandon our mission, we let go of our calling just because of a simple friction with some people.

In the text, Isaac had series of frictions with the people of Gerar his land of sojourning. Disputes and disputes over property ownership and rights. The people quarrelling with him did not know that it was the favour of God on Isaac that was coursing him to prosper in a foreign land.

You will be challenged no matter what you do as long as people can smell or see success coming your way. In the presence of God you are a winner any day. You will out wit others because of the word of God in you. Your source of inspiration is beyond the ordinary so you will surpass their intelligence. When they think they have backed you into a corner, they see you come out from another corner bigger, brighter and stronger.

God does not want you to give up or give in because you are facing stiff challenges. Isaac held fast to the word of God. He never left Gerar where he was told to stay because the people were hostile and disputed what he worked for and used his sweat to achieve. God is not telling you to quit. He is telling you not to give up the good work. God will bless you to the extent that the opposition will envy you for your achievements. Isaac planted crops in that land and the same year reaped a hundredfold, because the LORD blessed him. The man became rich, and his wealth continued to grow until he became very wealthy. He had so many flocks and herds and servants that the Philistines envied him (Genesis 26:12-14).

Don't give up. God will make you too powerful for all the negative forces of the enemy.

TWENTY TWO

PREPARATION

1. Ready yet?

The reason why it is so important for you to set and achieve goals is that you have a unique purpose that only you can fulfil, the question however is how prepared are you to achieve your purpose?

It's kind of like building your own house, something you had better not attempt without a clear vision of your goals and a good set of blueprints, or you may wind up with some extra doors or windows and no place to put them! God is the architect of your life. His Word is a blueprint of His hopes and plans for your life. Trust Him to help you set your goals. If you have a problem being focused and setting goals for your life, one of the best things you can do is to start writing them down, both short-term and long-term ones. It's amazing how your life can begin to take shape when you can see on paper where you want to go.

So be on your marks......................

2. The dreamer – contributed by Katherine Charles

Everything you dream is but one creative step away from its perfect fulfilment. Your words, your thoughts and doings are not mere expressions of your subconscious imaginings in the non-dream aspect of infinite reality. They manifest themselves physically unfolding in Divine timing like new leaves delighting to return to this biosphere within time and space. And there is no impromptu declaration; they yield at their own pace.

Worse than the dreamer is the disbeliever, the faithless and fearful who cannot see that their life is pleading and ready to be blessed by their vision of unlimited possibilities. Your life is unblessed in the realm or repeated illusion, and dead are the dreams of the distressed and self - defeated, so now is the time to embrace yourself, preparations have long past, now is the time to call into being the divine plan for your life, now is the time at long last to release and let go of past hurts and to embrace the beauty of living in the colour of your dreams.

3. What if you suddenly come across £1M

I was sitting in our living room one Sunday watching a bit of TV with the missus. She was watching a programme on home improvements and I had to join in reluctantly. I watched as this couple were looking around for a property and they had a budget of over a million pound to spend on their dream home. The couple simply did not look like a pair that had a million pounds to spend; they did not even look the sort any bank will be willing to lend that type of money. Out of my inquisitiveness I pressed the 'information' button of the sky remote and then found out that they had won over £2M on the national lottery. So that explained it.

Our phone rang and I told our friend at the other end of the line what I was seeing on TV. Then suddenly a question popped into my head. I asked my friend a simple question; "if you suddenly came across £1M, what will you do with it?" He pulsed for a while and then responded "I really do not know, I have never thought that far ahead".

I told my friend to ask me the same question, which he did and my response was rather simply put like this "I would buy the merchandise of the biggest consultancy firm in the world, employ a few people, and I will be the head trainer. I would travel around the world teaching about the philosophy of attitude. I would also start a publishing company primarily aimed at helping struggling authors like myself. Then I would instruct my wife to buy our dream house and ...."

My friend asked me if I had thought about all these before and my answer was this, "I think about my 'dreams' everyday so much so that I have put it in writing".

You see, no one knows when that angel will suddenly come like a thief in the night and ask you to name "just one" thing that you desire. This might be your one chance to get what you have always desired, one chance to make your dreams come true. What will you do in that situation? Will you spend the minute you have naming everything on your wish list or will you spend the minute going hmmm, aaaah?

This is why I want to encourage you seize from just 'thinking up' your dreams because as it is written in Habakkuk 2:2, you should "Write the vision and engrave it so plainly upon tablets (on your that everyone who passes may [be able to] read [it easily and quickly] as he hastens by"

Always remember, you need to have a plan for yourself, write it somewhere private and study it like your life depends on it. This will enable you to be equipped for the future you want to have.

TWENTY THREE

PROCRASTINATION

1. I'll do it tomorrow

On Saturday morning I was engaged in some vigorous exercise and at the same time watching musicals on one of the numerous Gospel channels on TV.

There was a particular clip that really caught my attention; it was a song by a young man which had a peculiar melody that almost anyone would be drawn to. I stopped my exercise to concentrate on the rather striking melody beaming through the TV speakers. Midway into the musical video, on inscription started appearing on the screen reading something like this:

> *"This young man had a dream from his youth.*
> *He desired to release an album*
> *He wanted the album to be a collection of Gospel songs.*
> *He worked tirelessly to achieve his dream"*

The inscription disappeared for a few seconds and then they appeared again reading;

"By the time the album was released he was with the Lord"

The video ended with the inscription:

(Singers name) 1972 – 2004

I was motionless for a few seconds thinking of the unfortunate loss of such a young talented man. Then I began to wonder if he had left any children behind – maybe, maybe not. I felt sorry for his parents and other members of his family. Then a rather interesting thought dawned on me! If he had not pursued his dream – what would he have been remembered by? I only got to know about him because of the legacy he left behind; because he was determined enough to fulfil his dreams; because he decided to stand strong in the face of adversary and any form of hindrance – that is how I came to know about the young man.

With this in mind, I thought about the dreams I have and wondered if I should continue to pursue them today, or maybe they could wait until tomorrow.

What do you think, or better still, what option would you take?

2. What has July done wrong?

Literally, just a few days ago I logged on to the very famous Goggle website. I was going to do a search on a particular subject matter but instead of doing what I had planned to do, I was spell bound and amazed at the new design of the goggle front page. I thought to myself, I am sure I was on this site last night, it was then the same old boring front page – so why the 'sudden' change. The irony of the whole thing was that I was going to write on something entirely different this week until I was taken aback by what beheld my eyes on Goggle's front page. To be rather honest with you the new design is not what really caught my attention, but the improvement to the links and the various new features that were staring at me from the moment I logged on.

So I wondered, why did goggle need to change anything about their website. Let us be realistic here, they did not need to this do they? I mean theirs is one of the most regularly visited websites in the world. They are so big that you will not be too wrong in assuming that the world needs goggle more than goggle needs the world. Just a few months ago they were involved in the take over of a multi national company that is worth millions in whatever currency you could think off. The word 'goggle' is now a household name and even though there are a few other search engines knocking about, goggle stands out as the pacesetter – yet they still went ahead to improve their own website.

While I do not subscribe to change just for the sake of it, continual improvement to your self is paramount to living a fulfilled life. I guess we all owe ourselves that much; and we do not have to wait for the great bench mark before we 'decide' on taking action.

Bench Mark!

Next year I will do this, next year I want to become that and next year all my dreams will come to past – however for most people, that great next year never comes. It never comes simply because the phenomenon of 'next year' has become more of a fanciful way of procrastinating any implementation of self development that you would have been better off starting in April of the 'about to end' year. What on earth is so special about January (apart from being the month when one of my sisters was born). Why is it that December comes and we suddenly wake up and start day dreaming of what we will become or what we will achieve in the coming year? What has July done wrong?

I made a decision over twenty years ago to see the 1st day of every year as a day of rest. Apart from when I worked as a security officer some years ago, I have always had the day off from work and it has been a time for me to relax, and catch up with the world of movies. Now that I happen to have a soul mate, we rest together while our daughters catch up with the world of Cartoon Network! I can afford to do this because my plans for self improvement were made at calculated times during the year, I did not have to wait for some date to change before I started working out what to do next.

Your developmental plan should be continual and changes to such plans are very much allowed subject to current circumstances. The now is simply too important to be left for the tomorrow that typically becomes another tomorrow. The present day is packed with loads minutes that you could use to look at yourself and ponder on what needs to be altered a bit; next December might be too long a time to wait, I think!

TWENTY FOUR

REGRETS

1. Much Ado – contributed by Ijapari Haman

Sometimes we have nagging thoughts that weigh us down; some of them are such that we can't even share them with our nearest and dearest. It is for freedom that Christ has set us free.

Stand firm, then, and do not let yourselves be burdened again by a yoke of regrets. When our minds are pre-occupied with how we've failed, who has failed us, who may be disappointed in us, what we may fail at, when we worry about things that may never happen, it all seems like much ado about nothing because one's mind is in constant turmoil when we have been told that it is for freedom that Christ has set us free, shouldn't we then stand firm?

Our minds are so important to us that they can either make us or break us. What we do with our minds, the thoughts that we allow to run through our minds are as important as what we choose to eat or drink. Therefore focus your minds on whatsoever is pure, good and kind so your mind is filled with the right 'stuff'.

Free your minds from worrying and nagging thoughts.

I wish you happy thinking.

2. Oh Dear!

Have you ever been in a situation where you did or said something that you wished you could take back, something that you sincerely regret – but you know there is nothing you could do to make things right.

I was in such situation recently.

My wife was out of the country for about a week and I was left to care for the children with the help of our lovely au-pair, Miss Gayle. This meant that rather than sitting alone in my study doing my reading and writing, I spent the evenings in the living room with the girls and Miss Gayle either watching TV or playing some games. One evening, the girls were watching Sound of Music on TV and I joined in – big mistake. You see, I have never seen Sound of Music before, so I thought it was a good idea to see what the fuss was all about.

Why does this man have so many children around him? I asked while watching a particular scene. Miss Gayle said, they are all his children –"his children?" How many does he have? "Seven", Miss Gayle responded – oh my God, he must have spread himself around a bit I said. Miss Gayle said "no, he is not that kind of guy; he had all his children by one woman". "Wow! One woman had seven children, she must be strong", I said. So where is their mum? Miss Gayle looked at me funny as to say, why haven't you seen this film before. Anyway she eventually responded by saying "their mum died". I showed no pity in my response when I said – "seven children, no wonder she died!"

Oh dear!

The look I got from my children and Miss Gayle drew a massive picture.

As if the whole I dug for myself was not deep enough, rather than shut up and move on, I asked Miss Gayle how many children she had. She stirred at me, and in a very low tone she said "eight!"

Oh dear again!

To say I felt horrible is an understatement.

From time we say or do things that we wish we could take back, but the beauty of it all is that we simply cannot take them back. This is when the need arises to confront the situation. Running away never helps and it could only make matters worse. There are small regrets (like the above) and there are regrets that hang around us for ever. Either big or small, the sooner we confront such situations the better the chance that there will be some form of remedy to the situation.

We cannot afford to sit around and sulk over spilt milk, but we can quickly clean up the mess and move on.

Show me someone without any regrets, and I will show you someone who hasn't lived. Show me someone who is truly fulfilled, and I will show you someone who has dealt with his mistakes head on and moved on.

Oh yeah, back to Miss Gayle; I told her she keeps herself well and more so, she is a good Christian, so there is no way she could die early.

Job done – I least I got a smile out of her!

3. We could all do with a clear out

I had to work from a colleague's desk recently and I could not but help noticing the amount of paper littering her desk. I took the liberty of having a quick scan of the stuff on her desk and it appeared that most of it did not need to be there. I walked around the office and I noticed the same trend on every desk, including mine.

I thought to myself, we need a clear out; however there was a problem. A clear out was not anywhere on the priority list of the team, there is hardly enough hours in the day to get our normal work done, so where on earth will the time to clear out the office come from? I knew that there was a lot to gain from getting rid of unwanted clutter and creating a tidier environment in the office; there was a lot to gain from a detailed and well arranged filing system; I knew there is a massive sense of 'being in control' to be gained from knowing exactly where information is when such information is needed – my problem was trying to convince the team that an office clear out was overdue. I walked around the office and got everyone to buy into my idea. I fixed a soon enough date and declared it the 'Office clear out Friday'; with the provision of 'free' lunch as an added incentive.

The day came, we all turned up in jeans and we dug straight into it. Lunchtime came rather quickly; we ordered food, sat around the table and had lunch together. After a rather enjoyable dinning time we went back to work and by the close of the day we all looked back on a job very well done. Everyone agreed that the task was very much worth the time and effort and we immediately saw the positive impact it had on us as individuals and as a team – everyone seemed be in better control of their workload.

That was the office – but how does this theory work in our individual lives, yours inclusive?

There is a limit to how far you can advance in life depending on how much clutter exists in your life and how much you are willing to de-clutter the 'de-clutterable'. It's like trying to send an email to someone whose inbox has exceeded its limit.

Mental clutter can give a sense of being overwhelmed, making us victims of unfinished projects; a crammed schedule which leads to having no time for ourselves and too many demands on our time from relationships that no longer serve us; to needy, negative people who drain our energy and the list goes on.

Clutter – it's not very nice.

Imagine trying to drive down a busy road with a windscreen covered in snow, or thick dust. You can only drive so far before you will have to pull over and clean your windscreen. Stopping and cleaning the windscreen means that time will have to be sacrificed and effort will have to be exerted; now this is where the trouble lies.

The greatest hindrance to de-cluttering our lives is the time and effort it takes to embark on the de-cluttering process.

You must have spent a few years on the planet, during this time people must have upset you, you must have been disappointed a few times, there is bound to be some past regrets in your life, maybe you have encountered a few failures that seem to have a stronghold on you, past negative experiences must definitely have had a part to play in your future endeavours, maybe someone passed a comment that has left an everlasting negative impact in your life. All this would have left a massive clutter in your life – and they need to be cleared so that you can make a move in the right direction.

You need to accept the need to de-clutter your life. If you cannot appreciate the positive effect of the exercise in the first place, then there is no point even starting. Why don't you take time off your normal activities for at least one day; go back in time and try and remember those things that you would rather want to forget. Think of the things you do now that happen to be a pure waste of your time and energy. Write them down and spend time pondering on each one. Are they worth holding you down? You have a good life to lead, trust me you do – but are you going to throw away the glory awaiting you due to clutter?

Go on, clear your head, clear your mind and start to live – clutter free!

TWENTY SEVEN

RELATIONSHIPS

1. Into perspective – contributed by Katherine Charles

I know that I am being watched. I have made up my mind to recognise the presence of God around me where ever I happen to be and no matter what I happen to be doing. This is why I need to guard my thoughts and actions, especially as I recognise that I am in constant communication with my God.

Like Iyanla Vanzant wrote in her book "Everyday I Pray"

"I am immersed in the sacred presence of God.
From the depths of my soul, prayers rise up on wings of faith and flow out into the universe.

What a joy it is to know that when I pray I am heard, and when my prayers are heard, they are answered.

In stressful times I will remember that there is an absolute calm in the midst of the storm. This calm is the sacred presence of God. It is there I want to be I now let my thoughts move toward God, knowing that God hears all, knows all and gives all. For this I am so grateful.

And so it is".

This puts my relationship with God into perspective.

2. Its official; I am overweight

Looking at it from the biggest point of view – according to the latest count, there is an estimate of over 6.5 Billion people on earth. I am not sure how widely you have travelled, how popular you are or how many people you have met during your stay on planet earth, but the most travelled and most extrovert person will probably have met thousands of people during their life time. I suppose the more people you meet, the more you get to realise how different others are from you, and how different people are from each other. Two people with identical backgrounds will turn out to be different from each other, never mind those who have come out of different environments.

One of the beauties of people is how different we are from each other; the worrying bit however is when we expect others to behave the way we do, or worse still – when we only associate with those who behave the way we want them to behave.

A major factor in developing a bad attitude is finding it difficult to accept that other people are not ordained to behave the way you do; or finding it difficult to accept others for who and what they are. Imagine for a second that everyone around you; every single person you know behaves the exact way you behave – what a monotonously boring world you would be living in.

Conversely, a major reason why some of us find it hard to portray a healthy outlook to life is because we tend to expect everyone we come across to accept us for whom we are, and then we end up petulant when we realise that we are not as popular as we had hoped.

I have learnt in sometimes a very unpleasant way that no matter how hard I try, some people will not necessarily be happy to see me around. This does not mean that they are not very good people; we are just different and maybe they cannot see the essence of my demeanour. I have also come to accept the fact that I do not have to laugh at your jokes when I find them witless. But more to the point, I know I cannot afford the luxury of eliminating the few people I come across from my life because I need them all. People come our way for various reasons, some for company, some to make us laugh, some to learn from, some to share our thoughts with, some to love and care for, some to make us feel popular, some to argue with, some to learn from, some for us to provide for, some for us to guide, some for us to mentor, some for us to show love and mercy – the list goes on.

Imagine me cutting people from my life because they don't laugh at my jokes (I can't blame them though!) or because they are of a different faith, or because they refuse to spell my name right (sorry to include this, but it hurts me!) - Then I might be left with no one to play with.

We cannot necessarily get on with everyone we come across, and we do not have to, let's not get hypocritical! We do however need to learn daily the importance of accepting people for whom they are and cease from measuring people based on some standard that we have set for ourselves. You cannot afford the luxury of assuming that Mr. Johnson will necessarily like you because you drive identical cars.

During the week I went to the gym and on my way out I decided to have my 'Body Mass Index' taken. The result was simply shocking – I measured over 25 (25.5 to be precise) which officially makes me overweight by 0.5 units. I wonder how many people will stop relating to me because I' am getting fat!

PLEASE NOTE: My weight is as a result of my bulging muscles – so don't get excited!

3. Next please

People come into your life for a reason, a season or a lifetime. When you figure out what reason each person is in your life for, you will know how to treat each person.

When someone is in your life for a reason. . . It is usually to meet a need you have expressed. They have come to assist you through a difficulty, to provide you with guidance and support, to aid you physically, emotionally, or spiritually. They may seem like a godsend, and they are! They are there for the reason you need them to be. Then, without any wrongdoing on your part, or at an inconvenient time, this person will say or do something to bring the relationship to an end. Sometimes they die. Sometimes they walk away. Sometimes they act up and force you to take a stand. What we must realise is that our need has been met, our desire fulfilled, their work is done. The prayer you sent up has been answered. And now it is time to move on.

145

Then people come into your life for a season. Because your turn has come to share, grow, or learn. They bring you an experience of peace, or make you laugh. They may teach you something you have never done. They usually give you an unbelievable amount of joy. Believe it! It is real! But only for a season.

Lifetime relationships teach you lifetime lessons: things you must build upon in order to have a solid emotional foundation. Your job is to accept the lesson, love the person, and put what you have learned to use in all other relationships and areas of your life. It is said that love is blind but friendship is clairvoyant.

4. The power of choice

You might have heard about the woman who was brought back to life just before her life support machine was turned off.

The lady was in a coma and the doctors came to the conclusion that there was no hope of her coming round; hence they were going to turn off the life support machine so that she could die in peace. Obviously, the lady was in oblivion of what was going on around her. She had no idea of the fact that the next time her eyes popped open, she might be in heaven (or otherwise).

Members of her extended family and some of her friends met the doctors for one last time and they pleaded to the doctors to carry out one more brain scan before the machine was turned off. The family and friends begged and begged and despite the reluctance of the 'brothers in white gown', the family and friends kept pleading until the doctors agreed to one last scan. The scan was carried out and there was a wee sign of life in the lady. In the week gone she was shown on SKY news celebrating her birthday with her family and friends.

Her divine recovery could be attributed to many factors, but ultimately it boils down to the people she choose to surround herself with. You could argue that she had no choice in deciding who her family members are; but you cannot argue about the fact that she had the power to decide if she wanted to be close to her extended family or not and she also had the power to decide on what friends to keep.

There are many choices that you can make that will either enhance or hinder your progress in life. One of the most important of these choices is your decision of what people you surround yourself with. Your closest kindred and acquaintances will always have an impact on how far you will head in the right or wrong direction of life. Your family is there to stand by you in times of adversity (trust me) but once you choose the right circle of influence, they will be there for you always (Proverbs 17:17).

It's important to establish the distinction between choosing friends and deciding on those you want to surround yourself with. If you want friends to socialise with, then go ahead and choose happening, popular people. But if we want friends to give you good advice and direction, you will be better of looking for people with a little more depth.

'The Power of Association' – a criterion to successful living.

There are various keys that serve as important indicators to what denotes a positive power of association, some of which include:

o   The need to include those who encourage your destiny. According to Ephesians 4:29 those you want to associate with are those whom no unwholesome talk come out of their mouths, but only what is helpful for building others up according to their needs, that it may benefit those who listen.

o   Do your associates treat other people well, because if they speak negatively of others; they will spread negativities about you as well.

o   How wonderful it is to hang out with those who sharpen you up and thereby make you a better person? Find them!

o   They better believe in your principle(s), otherwise you will soon be believing in theirs.

o   There is nothing wrong in choosing those who are not afraid to wound you because according to Proverbs 27:6, Faithful are the wounds of a friend, but the kisses of an enemy are deceitful. Positive criticism should be welcomed and used as a channel to improve you.

But most of all, always remember; these are two way systems and symbiotic relationships. You need to be a good associate to someone as well!

5. Who is your story

There are two types of relationships – the relationships that are decided for us, and the relationships that we choose.

With the first type of relationship, we have little input into deciding on whom we have special bonds with. Classical examples of these types of relationships include family members, school mates and to an extent your work colleagues. However, within this category of relationships you have the power to decide on what level you want to take each affiliation to.

In the second type of relationship, we have the sole power to decide on who will be included in our inner circle. This is where you have to make up your mind on which member of your family you will be forming a bond with, what school mates you will be keeping in touch with, and then you decide on who you want to share your joys and sorrows with – basically the second type of relationship involves nominating your true friends – how powerful!.

Concentrating on the second type of relationships, we usually have two types of people in our circle of influence, those that have the same reasoning as us, and those who we look up to. Conspicuously missing from our relationships are those classified as being less fortunate than us. We choose those equal or higher up than us as close friends because subconsciously we know that these are the type of people who could help us get to the next level – we also look good around them, seriously; who wants to associate with someone they classify as 'not good enough'?

So I guess you have made your decisions - and your friends speak a language similar to yours, they do identical jobs to yours, they have similar ambitions as you and maybe they encourage and inspire you; nothing wrong with all that. I presume every time is a good time to widen our scope a tiny bit by changing our attitudes toward deciding on whom to associate with. Maybe we should go to someone who would not ordinarily come to us. Maybe, just maybe we should say to this person, who might be less privileged, "please be my friend", then with all our heart, work with this person until they move up the ranks a bit. Maybe it's a good month to show love to those outside the clique.

Instead of being around those who make us feel good, maybe we should be around those who we make feel good.

You know what, by the end of February I will be forming relationships with at least two people who maybe would not ordinarily be in my clique, and I will be looking towards bringing them up to the benchmark that those I look up to have set for themselves. I want to contribute to the success story of a few, starting from this month – and I believe that the first and most challenging task is to form a relationship with them. When they are set on their ways to become even greater people, then at least I could point to them in the future and say "you know what, he / she is part of my success story'.

Do you think you could do this as well? Someone might just become part of your story...........

CHAPTER TWENTY-SIX

REPUTATION

1. Judging a book by it's cover

Have you ever wondered why some people light up a room as soon as they come in? Have you ever tried to figure out why some people get noticed easily and many others don't? Have you been intrigued by the thought that some individuals simply stand out?

I have always been inquisitive about what attributes mark some people out enough to make them stand out, Is it what they wear? How they communicate? Is it their looks? Does it depend on how intelligent they appear to be? Is it influenced by the amount of wealth they possess? Maybe the answer to all the above questions is yes, or maybe it's no – I really do not want to get into the deliberation. But what cannot be argued about is that we are all judged by what others think about us. And is it really important, I mean does it really matter what others think about us? Hmmm – let me think: Yes, it does!

If you don't believe me, just wait until your next interview and see if it matters what the panel thinks about you, wait until the next promotion opportunity comes up and see if it matters what your managers and colleagues think about you, wait until the day you decide to run for an office or position against some else. If you are of the school of thought that what people think about you does not matter, I wonder how you feel when you are intentionally left out of conversations, or when your name is 'mistakenly' left off the guest list.

What really gets to me is the fact that most people will make a judgement on you within the first few seconds of setting their eyes on you. Some say that we should never judge a book by its cover, however even those who believe in such theory do a bit of quick judging themselves, I am sure. This means that we all have a few seconds to impress; a few seconds to either make a mark or get forgotten. Just a few seconds to show that you are worth running to, or a few seconds to show that you are worth running away from.

The way you carry yourself may not be everything, however it could mean everything.

What will make you the man (or woman) of the moment at any time is not necessary what is worn, or what is driven – but more of how well you come across. People will react to a positive demeanour positively, and those who carry themselves around with a dropped head are usually treated negatively or pitifully at the best. It's in the posture, it's in the smile, it's in the right words at the right times, it's in the confidence, it's in the genuine care and love you display for others that will make you stand out from the rest. All these are what people see; however it comes from within. When you are truly fulfilled within yourself it shows on the outside.

Fulfilled?

Being truly fulfilled has nothing to do with money, fame or position. You could feel fulfilled even while you are in the struggle.

When you have a clean heart and hold no grudges against another, when you are free from the issues of hate or jealousy, when you encourage rather than put down, when you are positive about the future rather than being worried about the now, when you have a truly forgiving heart, when you find pleasure in the art of laughter, when you believe that 'you are the man' ('or woman') despite your issues, when you resist being put down by others – then you are on your way to being fulfilled. This will usually show on the outside, people will respond to you positively and when they judge your cover, it will always be good because your inside is of high quality.

Decide to have gladness in your heart, decide to forgive all hurts, decide to avoid the temptation of harbouring jealousy, and be as pleasant as possible. The result will be a sense of peace from within which will manifest as a more pleasant, more lovable and more approachable you!

2. No playtime for me tomorrow

I was busy doing some writing one Sunday when I saw our first daughter walking around with her head dropped. She looked very miserable and it was evident that there was something not right about her. Eventually I had to ask her what the problem was. "I cannot find my homework and I need to hand it in tomorrow at school" she said. Her mum, my lovely self and even her 3 year old sister spent a fair bit of time looking everywhere for the homework, and I honestly wish I could tell you that we found it; but that wouldn't be very true. I got fed up of searching and asked her what the consequences of the loss would be – she said she would not be allowed out during playtime and that she would also get marked down for not handing in her homework.

The next morning I went to her bedroom, kissed her goodbye and told her not to be too disappointed that she will not be allowed to play in school. I told her it will serve as a lesson and next time she will know better than misplacing her schoolwork. After my little sermon, I picked up the little one and off I went to work.

Later in the evening I asked her how it felt having to stay behind in class while others were out during playtime. She grinned from ear to ear and said "my teacher said I could go out and play because I have always been a good girl and this was the first time I did not hand in my homework".

Reputation!

It does not matter how much you may want to disagree with the concept 'what people think about you matters, a good reputation is one of the best assets an individual or an organisation could have; trust me, having a good reputation makes everything that you do much easier. Reputation, either good or bad is developed as a result of persistent particular action(s) over time, action which is usually manifested in words and deeds.

Reputation sticks because as we start off in life and begin to build character, we get labelled with good, bad or even worse, neutral reputations. If you are lucky enough to have developed a good reputation, you can usually get away with doing some not very good stuff while managing to keep your reputation intact – but I guess that will depend on what exactly you get yourself involved with, how many times the 'undesirable' action is committed and to how much the said action has affected the life of others.

This could be interpreted as thus "you could spend 20 years building a great reputation and then self destruct your empire in a few hours".

The most unfortunate aspect of this is where 'success' influences attitude'.

For many, the sorry situation is when they allow improved circumstances go to their head so much so that what they have achieved influences how they behave. Imagine, you start a small business and you are the happy smiley well loved shop man. Your reputation as the 'perfect' shop owner spreads wide and far and your small business begins to thrive and subsequently expand. As the money roles in, your good attitude rolls out. The old nanny whom you would usually greet with the warmest smile ever gradually becomes invisible in your sight and the guy on the other side of the road metamorphoses from a good neighbour to a bitter rival. Words start going round about the changes that are happening to you and your good reputation starts to take a dive.

Remember that your positive attitude to life might have earned you a good reputation, however; it all takes is one day and maybe one, just one dim action to destroy it.

The keeping of reputation is hard work, losing it is the easy bit.

3. Taken for granted

How would you want to be labelled?

Maybe before you answer the above question I need to let you know that it does not matter if you want to be labelled or not, it will always be irrelevant what your ideologies on the phenomenon of labelling people is, it does not count if you hide yourself in a cocoon and separate yourself from the rest of the world – you will be labelled anyway, so the sooner you get used to this fact the better.

So back to my initial question – how would you like to be labelled?

Maybe I could make this question a little easier for you to answer by letting you know how I (yes me, Ayodele) would love to be labelled. I would love to be labelled with my best qualities. I want to be known as the skinny guy who is putting in every effort to make his dreams come true and taking other people with him in the process. On the contrary, I dread being labelled lazy, unmotivated, direction-less, unfriendly or the guy with a bad attitude. There is a reason why I dread being labelled any of the above.

I believe strongly that once I take my focus off my efforts to avoid being labelled as any of the above negativities, then I run the risk of being given a label that I know I will dislike.

Taking your efforts in trying to become what you desire to become will put you at risk of being mislabelled. Your efforts (and mine as well) must never be taken for granted. You need to learn to cherish every step you take towards your destination. It does not matter how tiny the step is, you need to look back and give yourself a thumbs up for your endeavour. It maybe as simple as getting yourself up in the morning to go to work, you need to thank yourself for the effort in dragging yourself up and getting yourself to work, when you know you would have rather stayed in bed. It may be that you have started that business that you have always dreamt of; you need to look back and thank yourself for your efforts. No matter how big or how small, you always need to thank yourself and never take your efforts for granted, because if you do take your efforts for granted, you will sooner or later loose the will to keep on trying and then you get to be wrongly labelled.

It seems that even the obvious things in life can't be taken for granted. After a woman sued McDonalds because she wasn't warned her coffee was hot, companies started changing their instruction manuals and product warning labels to cover themselves from liability.

Some of these rather undesirable labels include:-

On a frozen dinner - Suggestion: Defrost before eating

A Christmas pudding - Product will be hot after heating

On a string of Christmas lights - for indoor or outdoor use only

A packet of peanuts warning - May contain traces of nuts

On a chain saw - Do not stop chain with hand

155

On a car mirror - Remember, objects in the mirror are actually behind you.

So; any answers yet to how you want to be labelled?

4. The electric chair – contributed by Ayoola Olusanya

In a trial, a Southern small town prosecuting attorney called his first witness, a grandmotherly, elderly woman to the stand.

He approached her and asked, Mrs Waters, do you know me?

She responded, "Why, yes, I do know you, Mr. Ade. I've known you since you were a young boy, and frankly, you've been a big disappointment to me. You lie, you cheat on your wife, and you manipulate people and talk about them behind their backs. You think you're a big shot when you haven't the brains to realize you never will amount to anything more than a two-bit paper pusher. Yes, I know you."

The lawyer was stunned! Not knowing what else to do, he pointed across the room and asked, "Mrs. Waters, do you know the defence attorney?"

She again replied, "Why, yes, I do. I've known Mr. Sanya since he was a youngster, too. He's lazy, bigoted, and he has a drinking problem. He can't build a normal relationship with anyone and his law practice is one of the worst in the entire village. Not to mention he cheated on his wife with three different women. One of them was your wife. Yes, I know him."

The defence attorney almost fainted with embarrassment.

The judge asked both counsellors to approach the bench and, in a very quiet voice, said, "If either of you idiots asks her if she knows me, I'll send you to the electric chair.

5. Who cares what you think?

There were two young brothers who were well known at school for their notoriety. One day the head of the school, which happened to be a catholic school, called the younger of the brothers into his office to discuss the brothers' rather unsavoury reputation. The school head asked the young man, 'do you know who God is?' 'Yes!' answered the young man. "Do you know where he is?" the school head asked. The young man kept quiet for a few minutes, and with teary eyes he ran out of the office straight into the arms of his elder brother sobbing and he said "God is missing and they think we stole Him"

A good reputation is not something that is achieved overnight; it's the product of persistent action over time.

A lot of people spend their days shooting their mouths off. But shooting your mouth off won't get you anything but a reputation for being a "blowhard." A good reputation is earned by saying the right things and following up with the right actions.

So what kind of actions will help you earn that golden reputation? More than anything else, you have to do the things that will affect people in a good way. From carrying Mrs. Aremu's groceries home for her when you were a kid to spending the night caring for your sick friend Robin; you understand! You don't necessarily have to do big things, but you must do a continuous string of small good deeds.

The thing to understand about a reputation is that it sticks. As you start out in life and begin building your reputation, people will label you with a good or bad reputation (some people have a neutral rep, but they aren't usually good for much, therefore there is no point discussing their pathetic case). If you have a good reputation, you can usually get away with doing some bad things while keeping your reputation intact. People may say things like "he strayed from the path," or "he had a lapse in judgment." Either way, they won't hold it against you for very long, assuming the behaviour was temporary.

The problem is when you get labelled with a bad reputation early on. Even if you go to church every Sunday and help old aunty Mary cross the street, people will still think you are a bad apple waiting to wreck havoc.

Don't ever forget: A reputation is for a lifetime.

Oh yea, before I forget – what people think about you matters; trust me!

TWENTY SEVEN

SELF DEVELOPMENT

1. Are you ready for it?

How many times have you heard people tell you what they dream of becoming? There is absolutely nothing wrong in that, however the question is how ready are these people for the actualisation of their dreams?

No matter how we look, talk or walk we basically have many of the same dreams. However, self-realisation may take many shapes. Depending on where you live, among whom you live and what opportunities are available, the dreams and the possibility of their fulfilment differ. This is why self-realisation tends to be both influenced by believes and by individuals. That means, individual choices and dreams are shaped by the way the majority think in a given society. One society may regard education and knowledge as the most coveted thing, another may regard money or material things as the highest attainment, and yet another finds spirituality as the perfect thing to strive for. Whatever your dream might be, the preparedness to live your dream is the true test that you will have to live by.

I guess this is why some dream to become leaders, and once their dream becomes true they struggle to cope with the task involved in their new role. Maybe while they were hoping for and dreaming up their hearts desire, they forgot to get enrolled for the appropriate training that would have given them the needed edge once the dream came true.

It was the first day of the fishing season, and a fisherman had just caught a huge fish. He tossed the fish back and caught another fish which was medium sized. He again tossed the fish back into the river and finally after trying again he caught a much smaller fish which he decided to keep.

A curious boy who was standing by and had seen the entire episode asked the fisherman why he had not kept the bigger fish.

The fisherman replied "Small Pan".

2. Good Works

Did you give your best at whatever you did today?

You can probably think of many times in which you simply did not give your best effort, or didn't really try very hard, lets hope this doesn't happen too often though!

Every person, because of our human imperfections, sometimes chooses to be lazy and not try. But the example given by Christ, and the one mentioned in Colossians 3:23 "Whatever you do, work at it with all your heart, as working for the Lord, not for men" is completely of the highest importance.

Resolve to be the best at whatever you do, because you should do everything as if you are doing it for God alone! When you put your whole heart into whatever it is you are supposed to do, God will recognise that and bless you for it. You should strive for and pursue excellence in all you do, for the sake of God; He blesses excellence!

3. Hidden Treasures – A story supplied by Mary Adelakun

I have a colleague who happens to be in love with paintings. Unlike me, she has a good eye when it comes to identifying good painting and she is willing to squander a few notes to get a decent painting in her home.

She recently had her flat redecorated and guesses on what she needed to complete the new layout of her flat – a masterpiece picture.

So, on line she went.

She searched and searched she found and found – she found nice paintings at very expensively nice prices; prices that simply put, she could not afford. This really broke her heart. Everything else was in place, the right colours, the matching carpets, matching curtains, matching sofas, even her light fittings had a design that went with everything else in the flat; the only thing that was missing – the painting.

She got back from work everyday and the first thing that struck her was the bear wall waiting for a befitting masterpiece.

One day she was woken by a light bulb; you know – the light bulb that comes on when a idea comes to you, the type of idea that makes you think to yourself "oh my God, why didn't I think of that".

It suddenly came back to her.

Many years ago, she was an A – student in Art. She won all the awards that could be won and she was at the top of the class in Art during her secondary education days.

So back to the internet she went; but this time she was not looking for a finished product. She went back to look for the raw materials, things like canvases, paints, drying oils, painting brushes, vanishes and all the rest. They happen to be cheaper than the finished product you see – but it's not about the savings; it's about the 'can do attitude'.

Mary happens to be one of the many of us who have hidden treasures within us. We sometimes over rely on 'finished products' rather that digging deep and finding out how we could apply ourselves enough to develop our own 'me product'.

When Mary eventually finishes her painting, it might not be the masterpiece that some Professor Nuts is charging a tonne of cash for – but when she wakes up every morning, she will look at the work of her hand, with her signature at the bottom of her own 'masterpiece' and she will be able to say to herself – "I did this".

And who knows; the right person might just pay her a visit one day!

4. Looking good

If you get to meet me, it might not seem obvious – but I do exercise regularly. I started visiting the gym over two years ago and even though the physical evidence might not be very apparent, I always feel a sense of accomplishment whenever I finish a round of exercise; a sense of accomplishment because despite my loaded schedule I still have the will power to ensure that I get physically fit. Still around the area of physicality, I consciously put effort into my colour combination anytime I have to walk out of the front door – I try to avoid wearing a blue top over a green pair of trousers. I regularly reduce the amount of hair on my rather big head and my nails have to always be dirt free. Based on all this you would think that I take a degree of care of myself – but who doesn't?

I am very certain that if you come across anyone who does not give a damn about how they appear, you would probably think there is something wrong somewhere. We all put in some effort to make sure that we look good, especially the ladies – and thank God for that, because a well presented lady makes me a very happy man!

We are exposed to a lot of judgements about who we are based on how we look physically, and more so how we appear mentally – mentally?!

Imagine; I walk up to you looking all good – a nice shirt, an expensive pair of shoes and my moustache well groomed. Then we are engaged in a conversation and you soon realise that my utterances are only as good as your twelve year old son's. You try to engage me in a dialogue and remembering what we spoke about a few seconds ago becomes difficult for me. You will soon walk away thinking 'good appearance, no intellect' – my rating with you will soon take a nose dive.

It's very important to note that your intelligence and level of education are very much independent of each other.

Mental exercise – a path to the ultimate level of 'well being'

I was talking to a colleague at work the other day and he told me something rather frightening. He once had a fracture and he was off work for two months. While he was off all he did was watch TV, eat, sleep and watch more TV. When he got back to work it took him months to get back to into the swing of things. He could hardly hold a memory for more than a few seconds, holding a thought was a task by itself and even his handwriting changed. Why did all this happen? – He spent two months doing nothing to engage his brain.

Brain power – use it or lose it.

The other week I was catching up with the news when an advert came up. A new game was in town, a game that engages your brain in some form of exercise – I hit the shops in a hurry and got myself one. I have to fight over the game with my 8 year old daughter but I really don't mind. I play the game regularly and I keep an eye on how my brain is doing. The first time I played the game, I was stunned by how old my brain was – it appeared as if I had left my brain in a state of dormancy for a long time. I discovered how slow I was to react to adding up, or putting a puzzle together. But at least I am now getting a bit better, I think.

We are living in a fast moving world, a world were brainpower is substituted for toys that do the thinking on our behalf. Look around you; gadgets are available to replace every mental function you can imagine. From sophisticated calculators, to satellite navigators, to spell checks on your computer (thank God for that though). You don't even have to read nowadays, just buy a CD version of a book and listen to it while you drive or while you do the cooking.

Apart form my new favourite game; there are other methods that are available to enhance brain fitness. From learning and memorising a new word everyday, to reducing the time you spend in front of the TV, to physical exercise and also laughing at every opportunity you get.

Brain fitness enhances wit, it makes us smarter and it makes us look good – consciously exercise your brain daily; it can only be good for you!

5. Take a break

We are sometime so busy trying to make a success of what we do that we get too involved and then forget to do one of the most basic things – taking a break.

From time we to time we need to STOP and reassess what we are trying to achieve, look back to see where we are coming from and re-examine where we are trying to get to. I have been so much involved in being a daddy, a husband, a church member, a writer (ha-ha) and a useful employee that I have almost forgotten to stop to look back so that I could hopefully see the future better and reload my arsenal.

I must confess; taking a break from work, seizing from thinking of how to sell my second book and spending time talking to people has helped me refocus my direction.

Once upon a time a very strong woodcutter asked for a job in a timber merchant, and he got it. The pay was really good and so were the work conditions. For that reason, the woodcutter was determined to do his best.

His boss gave him an axe and showed him the area where he was supposed to work.

The first day, the woodcutter brought 18 trees;

"Congratulations," the boss said. "Go on that way!"

Very motivated from the boss' words, the woodcutter tried harder the next day, but he could only bring 15 trees. The third day he try even harder, but he only could bring 10 trees. Day after day he was bringing less and less trees.

"I must be losing my strength", the woodcutter thought. He went to the boss and apologized, saying that he could not understand what was going on.

"When was the last time you sharpened your axe?" the boss asked.

"Sharpen? I had no time to sharpen my axe. I have been very busy trying to cut trees..."

TWENTY EIGHT

SELF ESTEEM

1. And he made himself big

The other week I sat in our living room doing one of the things that I enjoy doing the most – watching football. A replay was being shown of how one of the goalkeepers on display made a wonderful save. At the time the match was being shown live it seemed like the goalkeeper had made one of the saves of the season, however; when the reply was shown at a slower pace it became obvious that all that the goalkeeper actually did was make himself 'big'. I know that this is one area where I could do myself a lot of good – making myself a bit bigger, and so can many of us as well.

Jesus Christ is our perfect example of one who always stood tall. He is the one who personifies integrity, strength and courage.

Standing tall means

o   Being courageous in our decisions.

Once we have made up our minds to go ahead with a particular decision in our life, we need to stand tall against all forms of opposition and trials in making sure that we reach our destiny. Standing tall is fighting against all odds and getting the job done.

o   Not compromising our principles.

What can be said about a man without principles – everything goes, nothing stands. Today I want to serve God in all ways, however once the Pastor upsets me I will stop working in Gods house. I want to keep a happy home but I continue to go after anything in skirts. I want to claim to be of Christ but its ok to have a quick pint down the pub with colleagues on Friday evening.

o   Not violating spiritual principles.

The saviour said 'pray always and I will pour out my spirit upon you and great shall be your blessing'. It has been said that you reach your greatest height when you are on your knees. Profanity and crudeness do not exalt; they defile.

o   Not shrinking from responsibility.

Is our neighbourliness selective and confined to those of our faith, or is it all inclusive regardless of faith, colour or any perceived differences? To the saviour there was no reservation in the definition of the word 'neighbour'. Love of neighbour comes only after love of self and God and in order to stand tall we need to extend unequivocal love and respect to our neighbours.

Maybe we should try the above four 'standing tall' principles for starters and see how big we can get.

2.   Because I am worth it

I went shopping at the mall close to where we live the other week. I also had to pick up a present for my missus whose birthday was a few days later. Thankfully this time around she told me exactly what she wanted and where she wanted her present from, thereby saving me time and effort. I went straight to the shop she had 'recommended' that I buy her shoes from and while waiting for the lovely sales assistant to turn up with the shoes I decided to have a look around; and there it was.

It was about twelve years ago that a cousin of mine came for a visit wearing a particular pair of shoes and I simple fell in love with them. I have since seen them in various shops but I have not bought them simply because of the price tag. When I saw them again the other week, I picked one up and imaged myself wearing it to church on Sunday looking cool. I soon put it down, paid for my wife's shoes and walked out thinking to myself that I cannot afford them, at least not yet.

While I strongly believe in prudence, what would life be like if we didn't live a little? All this saving money, spending wisely is so important, but I will be the first to tell you that if you don't enjoy life, what's the point? Life is about balance and everything pretty much comes back to that. So, you've saved some money on grocery shopping and cooking for yourself; it's time to reward yourself a bit. Go out to dinner. Meet your significant other for a lunch date. Have brunch with your colleagues. Ask that hottie sister out to drinks or coffee after work. Its ok (provided you are single). You won't go broke. That is, of course if you learn how to splurge and indulge within your means.

A man was travelling in the Holy Land on a vacation when he came to the Sea of Galilee. Inquiring the price of a pleasure boat in which he might see the sights, he found it was £10 per hour.

"£10 per hour?" he exclaimed. "Why, I rent a boat in Cairo for less than half as much".
"Ah, but this is Palestine," replied the boatman, "and these are the waters on which the Lord walked."

"No wonder he walked!" said the man in disgust.

Oh yea, I went back to the shop, bought the shoes, and I make them look good!

3. Been here before

A middle aged man was walking through the park one evening and all of a sudden he heard a little voice calling, "help me, please, help me". The man looked around and saw no one so he continued his walk. Again he heard the voice saying "help me please". This time the man looked down and he saw a little frog just by his right foot. The man gently lifted up the frog and looked at it intently. Then all of a sudden like a bolt from the blue, the frog spoke. "I am really a beautiful young and extremely good looking and very caring lady. All you have to do is kiss me and I will turn back to my original form and I will love you for the rest of my life.

The man thought for a moment, placed the frog in his top pocket and continued walking. The little frog looked up in bewilderment and said to the man "why didn't you kiss me?" The man responded, "Frankly, after all that I have gone through with women, I would rather have a talking frog".

Each experience we have either shows us who we are or who we are not. We need to realise that the experience we have perceived as bad in our past and managed to rise up against prepares us to become a teacher to others who are going through the same thing as we did. The negative feelings we sometimes get from bad experiences also assist us in making better decisions the next time around, thus we feel better.

I guess it's time we stop beating ourselves up and putting ourselves down due to what happened some time ago in our life. It is way past time to love yourself and hold a higher consciousness and understanding for your own dear sake. This equally means that the next time you cannot find a good thing about certain experiences in your life, ask yourself if you have stopped to realise the wisdom, knowledge, clarity, strength and understanding that you have truly gained from the experience.

We can see not very good experiences as a plan for us to stand in all our glory and shine like we have never shone before. It is about time for us to see ourselves in a new light through the eyes of love. Stop putting yourself down and hurting yourself. We need to rise to who we really are and realise the gift that we have truly received from all those experiences.

I think most importantly, one question that come to mind is this, "would I allow the past incidents in my life stop me from trying again so much so that I risk the chance of losing out on my exceptional destiny".

I don't think so. Do you?

4.   Being exceptional – contributed by Kolade Isaac Ayodele

The truth is that truly exceptional people and truly exceptional faith (irrespective of whether or not one is a Christian) are revealed as problems mount and issues deteriorate beyond what is conceivable to the human imagination.

I think what made icons like Mahatma Gandhi, Martin Luther King Jr. and JFK stand out is steely, unbending conviction that there is a power in every man to create his preferred future. The present is only a journey, and the journey most times never truly reflects the brilliance of what lies ahead. Consider this: If you lack self belief, you can never truly believe in the God who believes in you.

5. Does anyone understand you?

A while ago, I got a phone call from a one time manager of mine who had just come back from travelling around the world. He managed me for about two years and we became good friends in the process. We worked well together and we would hang out together at the weekends and he got to know where I lived and versa visa.

He came back from a year of 'around the world' travelling and we decided to meet up and catch up. I obviously wanted to know what his journey was like and get to know a bit about the different cultures that he had come across. In return he wanted to know what I was doing with myself, especially career wise. I told him about my current job and what I was doing to move up the career ladder. I told him how much I have been able to develop myself in different areas and how I have been able to build up new interests, such as delivering presentations. I told him that I tried out my presentation skills a few times in Church and that I have also had the opportunity to do some at work and how this was fast becoming a passion. While I was telling this to my ex-manager friend I was beaming from ear to ear with excitement and a sense of accomplishment. This level of excitement was however just about to be punctured. After my ranting my friend asked me the simplest of questions 'so at these presentations at work do the listeners actually understand what you are saying?' – making reference to my accent. I tried very hard to avoid showing my disgruntlement about the question, I just smiled and changed the subject altogether.

I got home very late and went straight to bed still wondering if I should still be interested in delivering presentations or even standing in front of people to talk as I usually love doing. I told my wife what my friend had said the next morning before getting ready for church and in her usual way all she said was 'who cares what anyone thinks'.

Negative remarks – we should always be strong enough to resist them and go ahead with what God has in mind for us to do.

So who are those people who give negative remarks?

They are mostly people who have never put together a real product. They just talk a load of rubbish and say what is wrong with whatever they are ranting about. In fact they get a kick out of it. It makes them feel better to put something down as if they are better than it or too cool to 'jump on the wagon' and their ideology is backwards.

Personally I have no time for these types of people!

Do you know their greatest excuse is? – They are giving constructive criticism!

Personally, I do not believe in negative comments. Some will call them constructive, but guess what; there is nothing constructive about them at all. How about those unnecessary questions such as – why did you do this? Why did you do that? – They are in no way helpful.

Now that I have got that off my chest – how did I deal with my good friend? Very easy -

- o I started by deleting his number from my phone book as I do not intend to be associated with people who are the business of putting me or anyone else down.

- o I called a few people who had listened to my previous presentations to get a more positive feedback.

- o I went back to work to following week and asked my manager if it was alright for me to do another presentation on a different subject – of course his answer was yes, this meant that he must have understood me previously.

- o I did not allow his comment to stay on my mind, and I will continue to block my heart to negative remarks.

Neither my ex-manager, nor anyone else is big enough to stop me from doing that I want to – and I know that you will not be stopped by negative comments either; or will you?

6. It's good to have the feeling you are the best

It may sound like the title track from a 90's reggae album – actually it is, however; how good it is to have the feeling you are the best.

I was working as an Analytical Chemist many years ago. I used to be the first to get to work and one of the last people to leave, and while in the laboratory I used to work very hard. I guess I was very young and I had a lot of energy to burn so I would work so hard, or maybe I was just trying to impress being that it was my first job.

My then supervisor – Mr Matthew as we called him – was mysteriously sacked from the company and I felt so sorry for him. He had a family to support and his wife was very much unemployed. I knew he had no savings and no means of paying the next months rent on his flat – my heart was full of pity for this gentleman. So I went to his flat one day after work and invited him to my house to meet my mum who was in the employment business; hoping that she would be able to help him get back into employment hurriedly.

It was a Saturday afternoon when Mr Matthew walked into our living room with Mrs Matthew. My mum came out of her room and pleasantries were exchanged after I did the introductions. She was about to go into her 'getting a new job speech' when Mr Matthew politely stopped her and said that he had a few things to say before my mum did her thing.

This is a rough idea of what Mr Matthew said to Mrs Olusanya

'I have come across many young people during my time; however your son stands out. For such a young man with no apparent responsibilities he is punctual and regular at work, extremely hard working and most importantly he is ever so polite and respectful. He treats everyone with utmost respect and in return everyone loves him'

I was truly shocked.

To make matters worse, Mrs Olusanya (the mum) also went into one. She said among others

'He is the best son anyone could have hoped for'
The problem I had with these two adults was that neither of them; not even the mum had ever said anything so good about me to my face before. It would have been nice if at least once in a while I had been told that I'm not as hopeless as I had always thought.

Maybe I would have had a better view of myself if I had then dared to 'have the feeling I was the best'.

And so should you – because if you wait to be told how good you are, it might never happen.

7. Small car – Contributed by Bola Iduoze

I usually drive through a narrow road to drop my son at school, and it can be quite a challenge to get two small cars driving through at the same time. The challenge becomes even tougher when you have other parents driving 'big American style four wheel drives'. The frustration of having to wait for these people manoeuvring the four-wheel drives usually gets to me, particularly if I am in a hurry and many cars have to wait in line for these cars to drive by.

On a regular basis, I discover that I start moaning about it, or wont let the first one go by, lest others want to go very quickly and get stuck, creating traffic. One day, I told my husband about my frustration, 'all these American four-wheel drives! They are not meant for UK roads and I don't understand why people drive them in UK at all. I wonder why people just don't go for 1.2litre small cars etc'. My husband looked at me and said, 'Are you sure you are not becoming a small minded person?' I examined that phrase and gave it a good thought.

It is very easy to become small minded, it is also very easy to justify small mindedness and to dwell at that level. We become small minded in the things we do and the things we can even trust God for. Our small mindedness sometimes makes us think God's capacity and ability is small as well and it affects how we live our lives generally.

I remember the story of Gideon, when God called him, God said 'Oh you mighty man of valour'. That was the way God saw him, but due to all the things that are happening around him and who he perceived himself to be, he could not see himself the way God saw him. This self perception created a lot of delays and problems for Gideon, but Gods ability to work with Gideon and assist Gideon to overcome this led to Gideon having another chance with God.

A few things affect our mindset and make us whom we are:-

Our environment: The more you stay in a place, the more you have the chance of getting confined to that place.

Our culture: The culture of where you are will determine how you think. I was thinking 'English small cars' whereas I could have thought 'what is wrong with the American style cars!'

Our Association: The people we move with will determine how we see life.

If all these affect our mindset, then a change of mindset can only come if we change some of these and replace them with other things. The best thing to replace small mindedness with is, 'what does God say about me? i.e. the word of God. The word of God is limitless in its promises and it will change your mentality and your mindset about who you are and what you can be in Christ, as long as you get to know it, and meditate on it, i.e. think about it always.

Small mindedness will affect you for life, so the earlier you start working on this the better.

8. What's in the sky – it is a bird or an eagle?

It usually starts from the tender age. You show signs of being unique and then your parents, teachers and even Sunday school personnel do everything within their power to apprehend what they can only perceive as weirdness. When a child runs around, they are apprehended and charged by all concerned for being disorderly. The shame about all this is that by throwing away the distinctive quality that the younger ones possess we make them grow up becoming just like everyone else – ordinary. Even as adults, everyone wants to be like the other person. We might not necessarily acknowledge this but it remains in our subconscious to want to be like someone else; not allowing for any form of originality to develop.

If God wanted us to act in similar modes, He would have asked Joshua to be like Moses, but instead He said "as I was with Moses, I will be with you". Hence it was not a requirement for Joshua to be like Moses before he could lead God's people. God must have thought the personalities, different they might be, were both good enough.

Stand out and be recognised for your uniqueness!

When we dig down deep enough, we get to discover that quality which marks us out because only we possess it. You then want to nurture and develop such eminence so much so that it becomes your trade mark. I was given the opportunity some years ago to take the announcements at my local church, Gateway Chapel, and I took the liberty of 'doing it my way'. Some liked it some, some thought I took too much time, and some made it their business to tell me off, but guess what – if I had to do it again nothing would change, actually it will only get better or worse depending on what side of the fence you belong to.

Do you know who the Chief Executive of Southeastern Trains Limited is? I thought not. I worked for the company for seven years of my life and even I don't know who he is. Do you know who the Chief Executive of Virgin Trains is? Why does Richard Branson stand out from all the other Train company chief executives? It's simple; while the rest were having never ending, and sometimes fruitless board meetings in posh hotels, speaking the Queens English and sipping tea, Mr. Branson was trying to break some world record by flying across the world in some air balloon and his venture was covered extensively by SKY news and the BBC – it is such display of 'lunacy' that makes the guy stand out and not his wealth!

Identity crisis!

You will never reach your full potential until you accept who you truly are, until you accept your uniqueness, until you appreciate the fact that you are different. There is nothing wrong in learning from other people and being open to change - but you cannot afford the luxury of being insecure because someone is smarter, better looking or does a more fanciful job than you do. I have two daughters who are completely different from one another in all aspects – apart from the fact that they both have my good looks! I love the uniqueness of each one and I will never compare them or expect one to live by the measures of the other.

Once you love your own make up - tall, short, plump, hairy or bald; once you are able to identify what you can do better than anyone else (a fantastic matter of opinion); then you become an Eagle, and you are ready to take your place in the rather overcrowded sky. As busy as the sky is, while birds flock together in the same direction, to the same destiny, trying to decide on what to do next; the majestic Eagle soars on its own – it stands out and earns the respect and adoration of the whole world.

Be an Eagle!

7. Why wasn't I selected?

I was involved in a discussion with one of my senior managers just before we broke off for the short Easter break last week. Our discussion went back about 18 months ago when he was on the panel of interviewers that I faced when I went for a promotion. So, out of curiosity I asked him why I was not selected for the job, his response – I came across as too confident. Too confident, yes he said too confident. I thanked him for letting me know this and I walked out of his office with a massive smile on my face, feeling truly fulfilled with a massive sense of achievement.

Me - too confident, thank God!

I grew up being shy, timid, always feeling that I was not fit for purpose and with no confidence whatsoever. Even during my higher education I would find it difficult to make friends, I would sit at the back of the lecture rooms and wait until everyone left before I quietly sneaked out. When I got my first job in the UK, the wonderful job of cleaning toilets, I would walk around with a dropped head, literally. Even when I was promoted to a security officer nothing changed, and although I later got a more lucrative job, my confidence was still very much un-lucrative. This clearly meant that my status had nothing to do with my low esteem. I just had a low self esteem and nothing was going to change, even if I was handed a million dollars for doing absolutely nothing – the esteem was low and very low it was going to remain.

So I was going to remain negative about myself, then the day came, the day I decided to love me! And I do love me, I love me so much that I could talk about me forever (bored yet?), I love me so much that I could walk into any room and strike a conversation with anyone, including the 'finest' girl, something I would have never dared some years ago. I love me so much that I could stand in front of any crowd and deliver a speech, I know I can walk tall even in the face of occasional rejections – my God, I love the new me.

I hope you love yourself too, I really do.

Let modesty take a very high leap, if you do not believe in yourself, you have no right to expect anyone else to believe in you. The way you come across is the way people will receive you, your image will speak before you utter a word, and people will always respect those who believe in themselves. It's all in the mind and it manifests on the outside because your outlook speaks volumes.

So there were rejections, you have tried a few things out in the past and you fell flat on your face, you might have a few things that you wish you could change about yourself, you might have been laughed at, or maybe your past efforts have been overlooked and criticised rather than being praised. Trust me, you are not alone – I have been there loads of times and so has almost everyone else. I just wonder if you will be doing yourself any justice by concentrating on the unpleasant past, allowing the past to have a hold on your better future. How about the many wonderful many things that you have achieved? Oh yeah, I think I know what the issue is. It might be a bit more convenient to look back and see the depressing past or things you consider not to be right about yourself rather than concentrating on the little things like your beautiful set of teeth. Maybe some low life has made it their prerogative to remind you regularly of the mistake that you would rather forget. The guy you look up to might have through a dumb slip of tongue reminded you that you walk funny.

Purge your heart of all negative thoughts, remind yourself every minute of every day that you are a winner, dress to impress, make your home your palace, clean that car weekly (oops!), talk yourself up, pay the gym a visit, always sit in the front row (apart from when at the cinema), look at others in the eye, and laugh very loudly – and whatever happens do not throw away your confidence; it will be richly rewarded (Hebrews 10:35)

And with the job thing, it doesn't really matter. I'd rather have the confidence; other things will soon fall into place.

TWENTY NINE

TIME

---

1. Do as you are told; otherwise – Bang!

It was the late shift on a very dark and cold winter night. The Railway Station was almost deserted and I was all alone in the ticket office waiting for the next passenger to buy a ticket.

In the meantime, I was keeping myself busy by carrying out some emergency repair works to the spare, now phased out "All Purpose Ticket Issuing System" (APTIS) machine in the office in readiness for the guys on the morning shift. So there I was utilising my technical ability in ensuring that my colleagues came into a fully functional office, at the same time keeping an eye out for the next customer. At last, there was a knock on the window and I left the machine, greeted the customer with a grin and sold him the ticket he required. Once he left, I walked across the other side of the office to continue downloading and uploading data into the machine I was working on. After a few minutes there was another knock, oh well! Another customer for me to serve – or so I thought! I got to the window to see a guy wearing a mask and pointing a gun at me; and I did exactly what you would have done – Freeze!

While still 'frozen', the guy with the gun said, "if you try to move I will blast your 'flipping' (putting it rather mildly) head off!"

Yeah right! Like I was going to – remember, my legs were frozen, all three of them!

The next thing I heard was an instruction saying "I want you to empty that till and pass all the money to me and you better do as you are told otherwise I will shoot you". I wish I could tell you that I was brave and refused his

179

order, but I can't. He took the money, ran off and a few minutes later the station was cornered off by the police who carried out the usual ceremony that follows a crime. I was interviewed, or should that be questioned, by the police and my manager eventually turned up and took me home. She told me to take as much time as I needed to 'recover' and only return to work when I was good and ready. She said she did not expect to see me at work in a least a month.

If you already feel down and out and then you eventually decide to drain whatever life is left in you, watch British breakfast TV. After watching it for a week, and after being bored to the bones, I decided to call the office and tell them that I was resuming work. "No! You couldn't have recovered yet", the whole world, including my manager kept telling me. I was not having any of that; I went back to work to resume duties in the same office where my whole life flashed in front of me just over a week ago, despite being offered alternative offices to work from.

Was it easy for me to erase what had happen to me and go on as if nothing had happened? No! Anytime someone knocked on the window, or whenever someone seemed to suddenly appear from nowhere my heart jumped and I got really scared and sometimes I could feel my feet shaking with fear. For a very long time, I could not leave the office without some form of escort. I would sometimes be at the window and suddenly I will have flashbacks of the incident and all of a suddenly I would become emotional – I was basically turning into someone else. But despite all this, I remained at the same location and continued to work towards getting my old self back.

They say time is the greatest healer – I do not think so!

Time can help, but a lot more is required to heal past hurts, disappointments, tragedies, failures, loses, wounds and mistakes.

Why do you think I decided to go back to work despite not being fully ready? – Apart from the boredom that was strangling whatever life was left out of me; I needed to be in full control of my decisions despite what happened to me.

If I wanted to defeat the fear that was holding me back, I had to confront it!

To want to 'heal' the hurts of the past, you need to have the desire to heal it in the first place, and time is never a substitute for desire – however a combination of desire and time will always be the best remedy for dealing with whatever past issues that might seem to continue holding you back.

I looked at my fear in the eye, challenged it and allowed time to complete the healing process.

Will you be looking your own fears in the eyes and then allow time to complete the healing process – Please do!

2. That is my space

There are some movies that I can watch over and over again. I never get tired of such movies; actually they are the type of movies that remind me of what is written in Isaiah 35:4 - say to those with fearful hearts, "Be strong, do not fear; your God will come, he will come with vengeance; with divine retribution he will come to save you".

Movies that will remain in my head for almost ever are Movies like Ransom starring Mel Gibson; movies like Payback also starring Mel Gibson; movies like Breakdown starring Kurt Russell and Man on Fire starring Denzel Washington.

Of all the testimonies that I have heard at my local church one stands out for me; the one that shares a common ground with the movies mentioned above.

According to the lady who gave the testimony, she was living alone in her flat and next door was a very scary looking man who always walked around in a manner that made him believe in his own head that he owned the place. He was very unfriendly and intimidating at the same time. You dare not cross his path without a good explanation.

One day the lady came back from work and she parked her tiny car in the nearest available space she could find. She locked the car up and went into her flat to relax after a hard days work. Suddenly; Thump! Thump!! Thump!!! She opened up her door and standing there was this rather terrifying figure – it belonged to her neighbour. "You parked your car in my favourite space and I need you to move it now" he yelled. The lady knew the parking spaces were not allocated to particular tenants and it has always been a case of first come first serve with parking. Anyway, she wasn't going to argue with the big guy. She quickly grabbed her car keys, ran out of the house and moved her car to another space which was a few metres away. On her way back to her flat she saw that Mr 'My Space' had already parked his car in the space her car was initially parked. She got to her flat and continued with whatever she was doing. About five minutes later she heard a very loud screeching sound followed by a very loud BANG! She hurried to her window, looked outside and noticed a rickety car making its 'escape' down the road. She looked a bit to the left and lo and behold, her neighbours car (oh yeah the same one) had been run into and the entire side was badly smashed. It might have been her car if she had not moved it; or better still – if her neighbour had not made her move her car, he might have avoided the calamity that bestowed him.

The common ground that the movies mentioned above and the testimony described share can be put in a simple sentence - "I might look puny, but if you dare mess with me, I will surprise you with the hidden powers I possess – and my settling of scores will be almost instant!"

We can not all walk around with the 'don't mess with me demeanour' but sometimes we need to let some people know that we are not going to be slighted just because of who or what we are. However; some people might find pleasure in treating you shoddily just because they possess the power to do so and, and maybe there is not a lot you can do about it because you are powerless to take control of the situation. This is where Ecclesiastes 3 in the Good Book comes in handy. There is a time for everything, and a season for every activity under heaven, which means there is a time when you will need to fight the good fight yourself and there is a time for you to leave vengeance for the higher being to dispense.

One of the common mistakes that some of us make is that we lie to ourselves, lie to ourselves by telling ourselves that it is okay to be taken for granted. Once we present that 'weakness' to the world we are basically announcing ourselves as targets and we will continue to be undervalued until we do something to stop the undervaluing. The good news here is that there are only two options to choose from – you either act (provided you are big enough) or you hand the situation over to the Almighty God who has promised to come with vengeance on your behalf.

You need to know when to act, but either way – action needs to be taken.

3. The harbourage of insects – Contributed by Olamide Sanni

To know the value of one minute, ask someone who missed the train and has to wait for thirty minutes to get on the next one. To realise the value of one year, ask a student who has failed an exam and has to wait another year to re-sit the exams; to realize the value of one month, ask a mother who has given birth to a premature baby…" The essence of this recital, simply put, is that time waits for no man.

It is human nature to feel regret for time lost or wasted. The most painful thing about time wastage and loss is it cannot be recovered except of course by divine intervention and grace.

Many times, individuals' attitudes and characteristics either make them the locusts and cankerworms, or cause them to become a harbourage for these insects i.e. the tendency to waste time – which in effect does nothing other than to devour and destroy.

What are these characteristics?

1. Ignorance: Probably the most destructive insect of all. Hosea 4:6 "my people perish for lack of knowledge". Need I say more?

2. Procrastination: A ravaging insect that is also popularly called the thief of time.

3. Cowardice: The fear of failure causes many to refrain from taking the bold step towards redeeming their lost time. The fear of loneliness causes many to remain in unfulfilling and failed relationships where they continue to waste their time and their lives.

4. Lethargy: Otherwise known as laziness, indolence, slothfulness, idleness, sluggishness, it is more deadly than it appears.

5. Choices: Making the wrong choices regarding career, vocation, friendships, relationships, and all others may be the factor that sets apart a successful individual from one with an aborted destiny.

6. Lack of vision: The ability to look into the future makes one prepare for it. The inability to dream or live with foresight culminates in failure to plan ahead and as the saying goes;" failure to plan is planning to fail". Lack of vision can be likened to ignorance, and is just as lethal as the latter.

The foregoing is not an exhaustive list of the vices that make us a harbourage for the insects which devour our time.

Maybe, just maybe we need to look within to discover the insects we harbour as individuals and exterminate them once and for all. It is beneficial to avoid the loss in the very first instance, as prevention they say is better than cure.

Having said that, for those who have suffered loss of time through no fault of theirs, like the Israelites during their sojourn in the wilderness - it is very well to revert to Joel 2:25.

4. Where is the Bus?

I was on holiday with the family in France. Bearing in mind we could not speak the language, we had to keep to the minimal instructions that we could interpret.

Our first day out was hectic to say the least. It took us over 90 minutes and jumping on three different train services just to get to Euro Disney. After being subjected to various rides and walking around for almost ever, it was finally time to go back to the hotel. We walked with our very tired legs to the train station and jumped on the train, got off, jumped on another one, then another one and eventually we got to where we were supposed to be picked up by a shuttle bus back to the hotel. It was very late and the children were understandably getting very restless. We were not sure if we were waiting at the right place for the shuttle bus – and its non emergence got us even more anxious. I told my wife that we should get a cab which would have cost us a lot of money. I was so tired that I just wanted to get back to somewhere I could rest and get my thoughts together – and at this point; money was the least of my worries. The children were very weary and my wife looked fatigued. The taxi seemed the reasonable solution to our worries, so again I told my wife that we should get a cab. "Let's wait another 5 minutes" she said; and lo and behold, precisely 5 minutes later the shuttle bus turned up.

If we had taken a taxi, we would have got to the hotel at almost the same time, and with the same comfort as the shuttle – but at a greater expense. Waiting saved us a few Euros.

Waiting – the grace to hold on for a little longer and reap the benefit of patience.

When do we wait, and when do we hurry and get things done? When do we hold on and when do we need to make decisions and execute them snappily?

On a personal note, I am one of the most impatient people around; I want things done as quickly as yesterday and you dare not ask me to wait another day when I know you can provide a solution to my problem now. But is this the best way to be? I wonder if I would have had more successes in my various endeavours if I could only be a bit more patient; maybe I would stop getting on people's nerves if I stopped urging them to hurry up and get things done; I might end up having more friends as well. Maybe I should slow down and give some decisions more thoughts – or maybe not!

There is a time for everything, including a time to be patient and times to be very impatient. The patient dog used to get the fattest bone some decades ago – nowadays the other dogs have become a bit smarter. The real issue here is the ability to make a distinction between the areas in our lives where we need to be patient and those areas where we need to hasten to get things done. Where there is no clarity between the two, we end up getting our priorities mixed up; once our priorities are mixed up we give attention to the right things at the wrong times, or the other way round and once we do this it becomes easy to miss out on God given opportunities.

It is very convenient to use patience as an excuse for the lack of urgency. I met a guy a few years ago in the UK, and he invited me to a party at his home. I went expecting to see a large crowd of people – but it was just my new friend, two other guys, and about ten ladies who seemed ready to have

185

a good time. I asked him which of the ladies was his wife – he said his wife and kids were in Nigeria expecting to join him in the UK soon. He said his wife had been urging him to do whatever it takes for her and the children to join him in London, and he always wondered why she couldn't have some patience. Those were one of the times when I detested the word patience. I think what he really meant was 'My wife should learn to chill out and stay where she is while I continue to enjoy myself in the UK without the interference of my family'.

The only person that can really decipher what situations warrant quick action from situations where patience can be a virtue is you. The main concern is where patience is used as an excuse for procrastination. We need to identify what aspects of our lives can be put on hold and what aspects have to be treated with a little more urgency. Waiting for the shuttle as described earlier was a brilliant idea and the waiting was not going to cost us a lot, but if the situation involved trying to catch the flight back home – waiting would not have been an option.

There are three things we have no control over; the weather, how other people treat you and time – but at least with time we have the power to run with time or allow time run over us – decide wisely.

THIRTY

WORDS

---

1. I am beautiful

I took a couple off days off work one week so that I could spend time with my daughters especially as the older girl was on half term break from school. I was getting them ready so that we could go out when I asked the three year old girl how she was. She got up from where she was sitting, walked to the mirror, turned around and said "daddy; I am beautiful".

Okay, she might have some of the 'show off' qualities she inherited from her mum; but what really got me thinking was the fact that she believed in herself from that young age. I prayed fervently that the belief she had in herself remained in her and that her belief would lead her to living a successful life. But more to that, she did not just believe in herself, she was able express her belief in words, and that is what I pray stays with her forever, the ability to positively confess her desires.

The power of your Mouth!

There is so much you can do by continually telling yourself that you are able and telling yourself that you can achieve whatever you desire to achieve. Some call this phenomenon Positive Affirmation; which is said to be a positive statement that you continually repeat to yourself so much so that it becomes implanted into your inner self and then becomes a source of inspiration for your future endeavours.

Talking to yourself is not always a form of madness. It is more of a way of telling yourself that you have the will and power to achieve what could sometimes seem unattainable. When I was in the process of writing my first book, so many obstacles stood in my way and they pulled out all that could be pulled out to hinder my dream. One of the instruments that I used to overcome doubts was by telling myself, 'I am an author'. I kept repeating this, even in my sleep I would say loud and clear 'Ayodele is an author'.

Obviously, just saying want you desire to achieve or become without involving any form of action will portray you as insane.

"However; when you combine your drive, your actions, your prayerful life, your belief, your persistence with continual positive confessions and faith, which is the substance of things hoped for, the evidence of things not seen (Hebrews 11:1) – you are done!

Why don't we spend this week talking to ourselves, saying what we want to become or achieve. You can start by telling yourself this, "because I want to, I can see it (by faith), and I can achieve it" then by Friday, top all that up with some action.

2. It's mine to protect

It is all too easy for someone else to speak negatives into our lives; too easy. How much of these negative seeds do we allow to develop into that which dictates how much we progress in life? That is entirely the prerogative of the person to whom such words are spoken.

From taking misleading advice from those that we are meant to be looking up to; to negative comments being made by those we have considered as our friends; to rejections from those we consider brethren; to being laughed at because of some flaws we have and the list goes on.

You might know about the very well known gospel singer, Kirk Franklin. He had a secret that he kept from everyone he knew, even his wife. It all started from an early age – when he was just 8. To fill up his rather void life he started to spend his time watching pornography. Everyone around him had bigger brothers who had stacks of pornographic magazines and videos under their beds. All Kirk did was take a look one day and then he got hooked. You would think that by giving his life to Christ the addiction was going to gradually fade away – nope! How about after he got married; you would have thought that things would have been better? Oh well – it only got worse. The guy was busy selling millions of records, preaching the gospel to nations through music and at the same time he was keeping a dark secret hence living a life of hypocrisy filled with guilt.

Do you know what the real sad bit to the whole episode is? All this could have been easily averted if only he knew how to prevent the seed his then Pastor planted into his life from growing. The then pastor spoke 'death' into the life of young Kirk. According to Kirk, at the age of 15 he started to get serious about his faith and for the first time he decided to talk to someone about his addiction to porn. The person he spoke to was his pastor who listened to all Kirk had to say and then said "oh, you're young—you'll grow out of it." That was all Kirk Franklin had to hear; his Pastor had told him that he will grow out of it – but Kirk got hooked more and was living a life of deception well into his adulthood.

But he had to make a decision eventually; was he going to continue to live a life of deceit and insincerity fuelled by a rather careless word said by someone he trusted, or was he going to take an alternative route by talking to himself – telling himself that he is bigger and better than the influence of pornography in his life and that he could do the right thing. He eventually did the right thing.

A few weeks ago I was told that I was a bit slow, all because I carried out a particular task the way I saw fit at the time – just because the carrier of the negative remark thought that my judgment was not in line with what they wanted does not make me inadequate. I could have gone back home to re-examine myself, feeling pitiful, put myself down even further and hence kill off the belief I have in myself; but no – no way. You see I know that I am brilliant in all I do, I know I am self motivated and even the carrier of the rather unfortunate remark will need to put on their skates to catch up with Mr. Wonderful (me!).

I am not against being corrected or getting the right counsel; that's a good thing – but you should have the right dispensation in knowing when the carrier of the comment is lifting you up or putting you down. Knowing if the advice is going to add to you or leave you worse off than when you started.

A wrong seed will be planted in your life either intentionally or inadvertently at some point, but it is your life at the end of the day – it is your choice to decide what seed you will allow to grow on your fertile ground, it is your life to protect.

Decide wisely!

3. Priceless

I was tearing my hair out trying to figure out how to cope with the rather demanding task at hand.

We were on holiday and the missus and her friend had gone out to do that thing that ladies like doing the most, shopping. She left me at home with our two daughters for me to take care of. The morning bit of the job was kind of easy, especially as she had already prepared the girls' breakfast and she also gave me a ray of hope by promising to be back from her shopping engagement before lunchtime. However, lunchtime came and wifey was nowhere to be found. The kids were getting restless and hunger was evidently setting in. I could not hold out any longer, so I found myself in the kitchen trying to figure out what to cook for the starving princesses. What would you like to eat? I asked, pretending to be someone with a clue – after minutes of guessing, the idea of pancakes came up. So I started to mix, break, stir and fry. I was getting in a state because I was not sure if I was doing the right thing or not. The first set of pancakes was ready and I dished them out for my eldest daughter. She took a bit and said "dad, this is really nice, actually it is better than the one mummy made us two days ago – thanks dad". Suddenly all the stress and anxiety disappeared, all my kitchen endeavours became worthwhile.

The right words plus right time – A perfect combination!

Saying the right words at the right time could make a whole heap of difference to any individual and it usually has a dual effect, i.e. on both the one who says the words, and the one whom the words are said to. We sometimes underestimate how powerful the impacts of our words have on others.

A man woke up one morning with a huge hangover the night after a business function.

He forces himself to open his eyes and the first thing he sees is a couple of aspirin next to a glass of water on the side table. And, next to them, a single red rose! He sits up in bed and sees his clothing in front of him, all clean and pressed.

The man looks around the room and sees that it is in perfect order, spotlessly clean. So is the rest of the house. He takes the aspirins, cringes when he sees a huge black eye staring back at him in the bathroom mirror and notices a note on the table:

"Honey, breakfast is on the stove, I left early to go shopping - Love you!!"

He stumbles to the kitchen and sure enough, there is hot breakfast and the morning newspaper. His son is also at the table, eating. Uncle B asks, "Son...what happened last night?"

"Well, you came home after 3 am, drunk and out of your mind. You broke the coffee table, threw up in the hallway and got that black eye when you ran into the door."

"So, why is everything in such perfect order, so clean, I have a rose and breakfast on the table waiting for me?"

His son replies, "Oh, that! Mom dragged you to the bedroom and when she tried to take your pants off, you screamed, "Leave me alone, whore, I'm married!!!"

Broken table - £200; hot breakfast - £5; Red Rose bud - £3; two aspirins - £0.50

Saying the right thing, at the right time... PRICELESS

4. She thought I was clever

The class was full with young children who had come to learn from the teacher, the teacher who we all looked up to as the bearer of all knowledge. I was about 8 years old at the time but I will live to remember this day – the day a powerful seed was planted into my spirit.

So there we were, all of us sitting quietly awaiting the utterance from our teacher, an utterance that was supposed to impact knowledge to the young hearts who had gathered together on that bright and beautiful morning. He read a passage from a book and asked pointed a few students out to answer some questions based on what he had read. For some strange reason he pointed to me and asked me to give an answer to a question, which I did. Then there was silence – silence from the teacher and from my fellow students. He kept his eyes fixed on me and after a few minutes he said "I have never seen anyone like you, you are the dullest student I have ever known".

I sat down, and he pointed out another student and asked him another question – which I think was answered well enough, at least he was not told off.

The irony of all this was that what the man said meant nothing to me, as soon as the class was over, I was out of the class playing around like nothing had happened – but trust me a lot had happened to me due to some careless statement from my teacher.

I was not a bad student at this time, maybe average, but not terribly bad. For some strange reason however, after this significant statement, I was always the worse student in any class I found myself. I was failing with honours for the rest of my primary school education. I managed to get admitted to a secondary school and the failing tradition continued.

First year in secondary school came, and at the end of the school year I was told that if I did not improve I would be asked to withdraw from the class. Second year, I was the worse student in the class – officially – and even though I managed to scrape into year three I was still flopping all the way - big time. Those days the 'position' system was used to place students in order of how well they had done throughout the year. This means that I had been coming last or there about since the time I was told of how bad I was a few years ago and this carried on until my third year in secondary school. In my third year I read a bit more, but at the very best I was only just above average.

One day I came back from school holding my report card – I bumped into a lady friend and after the usual exchange of pleasantries she asked me how I did in my school report. "OK" I responded – "I came 87th". She asked me the number of students in the class and I told her it's a combine number of about 150 students. "WOW! You must be clever!" she bawled. "Really, you actually think I am clever? I was shocked to hear anyone refer to me as being clever; I had always thought the word 'clever' was meant for other people. What my friend did not realise was that she had just changed my life for good, for good!

For the first time ever, someone called me 'clever', a word that I never thought would be used in the same sentence containing my name. That was all I needed, that was the tonic that was missing all that while. I suddenly believed in myself, I studied harder than ever, believing that I was good enough. At the end of the first term in year 4, I came second out of a combined class of over 100 students.

I had fellow students asking me how I could transform in such a short time.

Easy! Someone had said the right words to me – a simple word that changed me for good, for good.

5. Short Words – contributed by Bola Iduoze

It costs nothing to speak kind words to others. If anything, it makes them feel good and makes you feel great for making their day.

Try speaking kind words or words of encouragement to a few people today and you will be amazed how much difference that makes to their day and yours! Have a great day and keep on being just that lovely person you are!

Like mother Teresa said "Kind words can be short, but their echoes are endless"

6. Who would you listen to?

'Sticks and stones can break my bone, but words can never hurt me' – how wrong.

There are something's in our lives that we have full control of, and thankfully one of them is making a decision on whom to listen to.

Because words are such a powerful and influential instrument, the way we receive them could be very instrumental in our failure or success as individuals. Just one word is sometimes enough to make a dream come to reality, and conversely just one word could result in dreams being shattered.

I have decided within myself to decide on whom and what to listen to, especially as I have come to realise that some people will never have anything positive to say about anyone or anything. Once I get to realise that someone is in the category of those who only speck negativity – I literally do a 'runner' from them. You see, I have been a victim of negative remarks in the past and I have allowed such remarks decide on my next course of action – which is usually 'abort mission'. Well that stops from now on.

The Apostle Paul used the word corrupt to describe a speech that has the power to tear people down, adults and children alike. In Ephesians 4:29, Paul writes 'let no corrupt word proceed out of your mouth, but what is good for necessary edification'.

So when someone decides to make it their business to remind me of the inadequacies of my style of communication – I will simply wonder if they get the message I am trying to pass across or if they are just being unnecessarily finicky.

Let us examine our speech habits for careless words, and then resolve to build up every person we meet. Remember, people need encouragers more than they need critics.

So who or what will you be listening to?

AND FINALLY

Always remember, a good Attitude will always breed a good life.